For Malinda,
the single biggest influence in my life.

# DESIGNERS DON'T HAVE INFLUENCES

## AUSTIN HOWE

Allworth Press books may be purchased in bulk at special discounts for sales promotion, corporate gifts, fund-raising, or educational purposes. Special editions can also be created to specifications. For details, contact the Special Sales Department, Allworth Press, 307 West 36th Street, 11th Floor, New York, NY 10018 or info@skyhorsepublishing.com.

15 14 13 12 11      5 4 3 2 1

Published by Allworth Press
An imprint of Skyhorse Publishing
307 West 36th Street, 11th Floor, New York, NY 10018.

Allworth Press® is a registered trademark of Skyhorse Publishing, Inc.®, a Delaware corporation.

www.allworth.com

Jacket, interior design, and typography by Fredrik Averin

Portraits by Aaron James

ISBN: 978-1-58115-851-9

Library of Congress Cataloging-in-Publication Data
Howe, Austin.
Designers don't have influences / written by Austin Howe ; designed by Fredrik Averin.
    p. cm.
Includes index.
ISBN 978-1-58115-851-9
1. Design–Psychological aspects. 2. Influence (Literary, artistic, etc.) I. Averin, Fredrik.
    II. Title.
NK1520.H69 2011
745.4–dc22
2011005209

Printed in the United States of America

*Reading times are estimated based on averages. Individual times may vary.

# INTRODUCTION

# 2.0 MIN.

Disclaimer: this book is not an exhaustive compendium of every notable author or artist or inventor or entrepreneur. It's really more of a random collection of individuals who have impacted me in some way—people I think most designers would probably appreciate knowing a little more about. I have avoided the most obvious icons (Picasso, Frank Lloyd Wright, et al.) in favor of the slightly more obscure (Rachel Whiteread, William Kesling, et al.). That isn't because I don't find inspiration in the Picassos and the Frank Lloyd Wrights of the world. I most certainly do. But I assume that you are familiar enough with these luminaries to have already wrung inspiration from their lives and work. Instead, I have chosen each minibiography based on some qualitative aspect of the person's life or work that might inform or inspire some aspect of your life or work. My basic premise is that we can often learn more from people in other disciplines than we can from those in our own. *Designers Don't Have Influences* puts this premise to the test: can a creative person learn anything from a nun or a professional hockey coach? We'll soon find out.

Another decision that was made regarding this volume was to stay consistent with the format of *Designers Don't Read*—that is, no work samples. There were two reasons for this. One: designers do read. However, if they are good, they are busy, and often don't have time to sit down and invest huge chunks of time in dry, academic reading. That's why we have provided the average time it will take to read each chapter, as we did in *Designers Don't Read*. If you have a ten-minute window of time between your chopped salad and your next meeting, you can find a ten-minute chapter, and so on. Two: designers are often criticized (usually by advertising people) for indulging only in eye candy.

Monographs, award annuals, and the like. Well, the Designers Don't series follows in the spirit and tradition of Norman Potter's little gem, *What Is a Designer?*, which is 175 pages without a single image—not even a graph. That said, we've added the odd little discoverable just because. Which, by the way, is one of my favorite rationales for anything.

Once again, thanks to my dear friend and designer of the Designers Don't series, Fredrik Averin, for his daily inspiration and encouragement and amazingness. Thanks also to Tad Crawford, for his constant support, and to Claire Abramowitz for making me more legit (and for letting me use the word "amazingness").

# RACHEL WHITEREAD AND THE BEAUTY OF NEGATIVE SPACE

# 2.0 MIN.

Rachel Whiteread inspires me to approach projects differently. I assume that you are familiar with her work. She was one of the so-called YBAs (Young British Artists) made infamous by my former employer, Charles Saatchi, along with Damien Hirst, Tracey Emin, and Jenny Saville, at his swanky Saatchi Gallery in London. Her best-known piece was *House*, which was an actual Victorian house in east London that she filled with dental plaster and then had all the wood stripped away—leaving only the negative space of the house intact. She did similar pieces with entire rooms, staircases, bookshelves, cupboards, and desks, also using rubber and resin in addition to plaster.

*House* was awe-inspiring as an "event," but the beauty of her unique vision didn't really hit me until I sat staring at her bookshelf and desk installations. Looking at the solid form of space under a desk made me see that area my legs and feet have occupied for most of my life—for the very first time. The bookshelves really messed with my mind, seeing the space that my books actually occupy.

I like to encourage creative people to "walk all around an idea" to find different ways of approaching it. But Rachel Whiteread added another dimension to that exploration. Namely, turn the idea inside out. Look at what is already there and explore that. Heady stuff, but totally useful when you're reaching for a different way of communicating an idea.

Bottom line, her work inspires me to help people see things that they have looked at over and over again, in a whole new way. Things that may have been there all along. The courage of her vision ("I think I want to fill an entire house with dental plaster and remove the exterior of the house to reveal the negative space") earned her the prestigious Turner Prize for best young British artist (the first woman to receive that honor). But it also earned her derision and pushback and the K Foundation art award for "worst British artist." All in the same year.

Reminds me a bit of one of my favorite creative directors, who said of a global fashion campaign he's currently working on: "It doesn't look 'designed,' and we may miss on this—not sure." That degree of creative risk-taking is what separates great from good, inspirational from tried-and-true.

# ~~IAN SCHRAGER: WHAT HAPPENS TO A VISION WHEN THE VISIONARY MOVES ON?~~

# 3.0 MIN.

I have to admit that I was a bit melancholy when Ian Schrager quietly and gradually began unloading his Morgans Hotel properties. The Paramount was the first to go, followed by Morgans (his first hotel—whence came the name of the parent company), Hudson and Royalton in New York, the amazing Delano in Miami, St. Martin's Lane and Sanderson in London, Mondrian in West Hollywood, and my personal favorite: the Clift in San Francisco.

It marked the end of an era. But that's the inspiring thing.

Schrager, in his early sixties, is embarking on the third phase of his storied career (you may recall that his first incarnation was as co-owner of Studio 54 in New York). Now he's "breaking with his immediate past," as Adam Morgan would put it, and focusing on residences and hotels with a different, more refined, more artful vibe—working with his pal Julian Schnabel in lieu of pop designer and long-time collaborator Philippe Starck. He also engaged Herzog & de Meuron to work on 40 Bond, a residential project in New York. They're the ones who designed that incredible Prada building in Tokyo. Schrager says he "won't return to the familiar ground of design-centric boutique hotels. There are fake Starcks all over the place." I love that as soon as companies like Westin and others start copying his vision, he jettisons everything and starts over. I also love that he calls those hotels "Starcks" and not "Schragers." He gives props to his designer.

I'd recommend paying a visit to ianschragercompany.com. You can see some of his latest projects, and there are a few choice Schragerisms, including: "Lifestyle is the way a person distinguishes himself or herself. It is the artistry of living."

21

There are four things in particular that inspire me about Ian Schrager:

1.  He is an authentic, trailblazing visionary, a prime mover—not a follower.

2.  He almost single-handedly elevated the whole concept of travel and hotels.

3.  He is a fan, a patron, and a missionary of great design.

4.  He did jail time (with Studio 54 partner Steve Rubell, for tax evasion).

I was fortunate enough to experience Schrager's most recent hotel concept firsthand on a recent trip to New York. The Gramercy Park Hotel is, for my money, the new benchmark for luxury hotels, at least here in the United States. Every detail has been carefully considered—right down to the thermostats in the rooms and the "Do Not Disturb" signs hanging gracefully on the doors. The hotel also has its own branded scent, developed by Le Labo in New York. That, together with the pine logs burning in the lobby's massive fireplace and the masterfully curated original art and custom furniture, makes for a memorable stay. Or even just a memorable drink at the bar.

So, apparently, this is what happens when a visionary moves on: he takes his vision with him and then improves upon it.

# THE SAATCHIS: LOVE 'EM OR HATE 'EM, YOU HAVE TO RESPECT 'EM

# 3.0 MIN.

In 1988, I was a junior copywriter at Saatchi & Saatchi in Los Angeles. I was absolutely fascinated with the founders of the company, Charles and Maurice Saatchi, sons of an Iraqi Jew who immigrated to London in 1947. Driven by their simple credo, "Nothing is impossible," the Brothers—as they were (not so) affectionately known—were on an agency acquisition spree that would change the face of modern advertising, and ultimately (unbeknownst to me at the time) my own career as well. They used the stock market to fund the acquisitions of Backer & Spielvogel, Dancer Fitzgerald Sample, and Ted Bates, forming the world's largest advertising agency. This was the same agency that, just ten years prior, had felt so self-conscious about their tiny stature that they commissioned a designer to create an identity that would make the nascent firm "seem more like a bank than a communications company." The decidedly "stable" Saatchi & Saatchi logo remains to this day. The founders do not.

By the time I was in their employ, they had already spent $1 billion to acquire thirty-seven companies and had eighteen thousand employees in five hundred offices in sixty-five countries. Simultaneously, Charles, a copywriter by training, had amassed one of the largest modern art collections in the world.

After a much-criticized (and unsuccessful) bid to buy U.K.-based Midland Bank, Saatchi & Saatchi began to hemorrhage cash. An American investor started buying up Saatchi shares and eventually led a charge to sack the Brothers, which culminated in Charles and Maurice and three other key executives leaving the agency they had founded to launch M&C Saatchi. (They wanted to call it "New Saatchi" but their previous firm's lawyers prevailed on the grounds that the name implied that the now Saatchi-less Saatchi & Saatchi was "Old Saatchi.")

More than a decade has passed, and Saatchi & Saatchi has maintained and possibly even surpassed the creative reputation it had when the Brothers were there. M&C Saatchi has become one of the U.K.'s finest creative agencies, with domestic billings exceeding Saatchi & Saatchi's and offices in thirteen countries. More importantly, their work is generally simple, smart, and beautiful—they are very close to our hybrid model, without making a fuss about it. My theory is that Charles's art fixation pushes the agency in that direction by default.

And me? Well, I fell prey to the Saatchi's merger and acquisition mania of the '90s and opted to sell my agency to a larger concern in 1996. But that allowed me to do what I'm doing now. So it appears that there are happy endings for everyone in this story. Saatchi & Saatchi is thriving, Maurice and Charles have risen like the proverbial phoenix from the ashes, and M&C Saatchi is turning out great work.

True, Maurice was one of the first to champion the notion of globalization, which has had significant consequences on our world. True, they did make out like bandits while other shareholders suffered during the Saatchi & Saatchi debacle. And true, Charles Saatchi has essentially become the art world's puppet master, controlling the fluctuation of the art market by buying up young artists' work, promoting them, and then selling them off. He is basically an art speculator, but there's no law against that. In fact, artists like Damien Hirst, Tracey Emin, and others are somewhat in his debt, if not in his very small circle of friends.

So, what is the lesson of the Brothers for me? Set your sights on something, stay focused on the goal, and nothing is impossible. Even the second time around.

# MATT HAIMOVITZ AND THE LATENT POWER OF BOREDOM

# 3.0 MIN.

Note: When I refer to someone as a beast, it's actually a compliment.
A beast is someone I find to be ridiculously talented, competent,
and visionary.

Matt Haimovitz is one such beast. First, check out his resume: he was
born in Israel, moved to the United States, and started studying cello with
Gabor Rejto at the ripe old age of seven. If the name Gabor Rejto doesn't
ring a bell, maybe his cello teacher's name will: Pablo Casals. At age
twelve, Haimovitz was studying with Itzhak Perlman, who—along with
Yo-Yo Ma—is probably the most famous living cellist. Perlman introduced
him to Leonard Rose at the Juilliard School in New York, where he
studied until he started touring with the Israel Philharmonic Orchestra
and later with the New York Philharmonic, and pretty much every other
kick-ass orchestra on the planet. At seventeen, Haimovitz, signed his first
record deal. But it wasn't until after he graduated from Harvard in 1996
that Matt Haimovitz started moving into even more beastly territory.

Bored and dissatisfied with the traditional career of a classical musician,
Haimovitz started to mix things up a bit. First he started messing with the
venue for his music: doing gigs in bars, rock and jazz clubs, coffee
houses, and outdoor festivals. Then, during his Anthem tour in 2003, he
started tinkering with musical genres, performing his own arrangement of
Jimi Hendrix's "Star-Spangled Banner" and collaborating with musicians
like John McLaughlin, DJ Olive, and Constantinople (a five-member
Middle Eastern band). One of his most recent albums is *After Reading
Shakespeare*, a virtuoso storytelling experiment interpreting works from
Shakespeare and Mark Twain. I'm listening to it as I write these words.

In 2000, Haimovitz cofounded Oxingale Records with his wife, composer Luna Pearl Woolf. The *New York Times* referred to Oxingale as one of music's "adventurous smaller companies where the real action has moved to." If "neoclassical" gets some traction toward becoming a serious new musical genre, my guess is that Matt Haimovitz and Oxingale will be at the forefront of it.

Haimovitz plays a Venetian cello that was made in 1710. One of the highlights of a recent West Coast tour (with his new cello ensemble, Uccello), was a cover of Led Zeppelin's "Kashmir," with the cellists slapping the bodies of their instruments and clacking their bows against the strings below the bridge to lay down the rhythm, and Haimovitz playing the vocal lines and Jimmy Page's guitar solos on his three-hundred-year-old instrument.

What inspires me most about Haimovitz's work is that there is a deep knowledge of and respect for the past (I think he was actually quoted once as saying that he "started out as a modernist"). But there is also his restlessness with the media and the forms that his artistry takes. He is mixing, blending, fusing. He is a musical "hybrid" and a model for our industry.

# DAMIEN HIRST IS NOT LAUGHING WITH YOU, HE'S LAUGHING AT YOU

# 4.0 MIN.

Note: The following contains frequent use of the word "ASSHOLE."
If the word "ASSHOLE" and/or the imagery that "ASSHOLE" connotes
are offensive to you in any way, I apologize in advance. The truth is,
"ASSHOLE" is the best, and in fact, the only word that aptly describes
the subject of this chapter.

Damien Hirst is one of those people I admire for being a completely
transparent asshole. By that I mean that he's not trying to hide the fact
that he's an asshole. In fact, he's trying so hard to convince you that he
is an asshole that after a while you genuinely start to like the chap.
Completely contradictory, self-important, dismissive of all influences
(except chemical ones), opinionated to the extreme, arrogant, self-
destructive, profane—and those are his best features. No, actually his
best features are his fearlessness, his childlike curiosity, his raw honesty,
his penchant for mischief, and his endearing respect for art and blatant
disregard for everything else—including "the art world." Exceptions:
Francis Bacon, his wife Maia, and his three sons, Connor, Cassius,
and Cyrus.

Hirst is best known for *The Physical Impossibility of Death in the Mind of
Someone Living*, a shark suspended in a vitrine filled with formaldehyde.
His other signature pieces include *A Thousand Years*, which is another
vitrine, this time with a decomposing cow's head covered with hatching
flies that eventually get zapped in an electric fly trap. Birth, life, and
death—it's all there. And decomposition. And the accompanying odor,
which forced him to resort to a fake head when gallery goers started
complaining about the stench. But it's that kind of human reaction to
his work that Hirst is actually going for. In his Pharmacy series, which
ranges from ironic pharmaceutical posters and packaging to steel

33

cases full of thousands of different pills to an actual pharmacy installation, you see his mischief and the ultimate aim of his art—when people got off the elevator at the gallery to see *Pharmacy*, many felt that they had actually stumbled into the wrong place and would go right back down the elevator. "Fantastic," Hirst would say with his characteristic impish glee. That is just the kind of human response that he is after. (He eventually opened a bar and restaurant called Pharmacy that was essentially an installation with fine dining.) Similarly, his *Spots* paintings could be construed as just Damien being Damien, but in reality, his motivation for *Spots* is—purely and simply—that he loves color, is ace at color, and wants people to be able to have all these amazing colors to brighten up their living rooms. A different kind of reaction. The seeming obsession with death in much of his work may stem from some painful exposure to the subject in his formative years, but it comes off as a bit of a celebration of life. Another major Hirst work is *Hymn*, a giant, six-ton bronze reproduction of one of his sons' toys.

As prolific as Andy Warhol and probably far richer for it, Hirst is a beast on a couple of levels, but he does inspire me to be fearless in my work, to be honest about exactly where I'm at in real time, and to let that be the basis of my writing. And to always aim for a human reaction.

I often challenge creative people to think about what it is they want to do with a project, not what they want to say. I suspect that some of my favorite designers are encouraged in similar and different ways—to find their unique voice and vision, as Hirst has. Anyone could have bought a shark and have it placed in a glass box full of formaldehyde, but Hirst did it first. He got there first and anyone who does anything like that now would be seen to be copying him. Anything in a glass box would be seen as Hirst-like. Same with the spots. Same with the huge brass sculptures. Or his skulls (although I just saw a piece that Jim Riswold did as an homage to Hirst: a skull covered in candy sprinkles like you'd find on a Voodoo doughnut).

I also like how he keeps changing it up and playing against what people expect from "Damien Hirst." Recently, he's turned his attention toward religious iconography.

Damien Hirst may be an asshole. But at least he's a talented, visionary, courageous, honest, and forgivable asshole.

# WHAT HOWARD HUGHES TAUGHT ME ABOUT GRAPHIC DESIGN

# 4.0 MIN.

For some inexplicable reason, I have always had a fascination with the person of Howard Robard Hughes, Jr. And with the word "inexplicable."

When I was a freshman at King George Secondary School in Vancouver, Canada, it was widely held that Hughes was occupying the penthouse of the Bayshore Inn, just three blocks from my school. I subsequently read every biography (and fake biography) I could get my hands on and started collecting Hughes memorabilia and rare recorded interviews. When I opened a recording studio in Hollywood in 1999, my building was just two doors down from Hughes's former command center at 7000 Romaine Street. When I discovered the coincidence, I went and met my new neighbors—a cold storage company. (Note: This was six years before the building appeared in Scorsese's *The Aviator*.) When I explained my obsession with Hughes, the manager asked me if I would like a tour of the facility. "Um, yes please." For some inexplicable legal reason, Howard's personal belongings still filled the basement vaults of his former offices. An old hand-painted Trans World Airlines map (Hughes owned TWA). The original film prints of *Scarface*. One room with nothing but his old aviation trophies. One with his old clothes, shoes, and unopened gifts. The manager later told me that "the Mormons" (Bill Gay and his so-called "Mormon mafia," who had run Hughes's operation and, some insist, effectively assisted the old man's gradual slide into drug addiction and madness) had recently come and poured out the pre-Prohibition liquor that Hughes's father used to give to presidents and film stars. The value of that hooch must have been practically incalculable.

I was inordinately happy when Hughes's H-4 wooden seaplane made its way from Long Beach Harbor to the Evergreen Aviation Museum in McMinnville, just fifteen minutes from my home in Portland. Having

37

donated some of my Hughes memorabilia to the museum, I was invited to see the "Spruce Goose" (Hughes disliked that name) before it was fully reassembled. It was an awesome sight, just as it had been when I first visited it in California.

Okay, I should probably get to the part where I learned something about graphic design from Howard Hughes. Actually, seen through my oddly respectful and compassionate lens, Hughes's life taught me about more than just graphic design, but about work and life in general. Here's a guy who is orphaned at seventeen, suddenly finds himself responsible for his deceased father's Hughes Tool Company, and moves to Hollywood to produce movies—including *Hell's Angels*, the original *Scarface*, and *The Outlaw*. Then he decides to focus on his other great love: flying. He designs and builds the Hughes H-1 Racer, sets several world records, including a trip around the world in just ninety-one hours (this was in 1938), beating the previous record by four days. Then Hughes designs quite possibly the most beautiful plane ever built, the XF-11 reconnaissance plane—which he crashes into a Beverly Hills neighborhood, breaking nearly every bone in his body and causing him to suffer terrible burns. Somehow, he recovers from this crash and three other near-fatal crashes. Who walks away from four plane crashes? But Hughes does, and doggedly pursues his vision for the flying boat as a solution to the problem of American losses on U.S. ships being torpedoed by German U-boats. The idea of the H-4 Hercules was to stay just far enough off the water so that U-boats couldn't sink it. Then Hughes buys and saves TWA. Buys and saves RKO Pictures, a film production and distribution company. Reinvents himself as a hotelier in Las Vegas, buying up most of the town long before "What happens in Vegas stays in Vegas." Racked with chronic pain throughout his entire body, Hughes becomes addicted to pain medication and withdraws from public life, but somehow still manages to envision and establish the Howard Hughes Medical Institute, which, with an endowment of $16.3 billion, has become America's largest private foundation devoted to biological and medical research. And I didn't even mention his romantic conquests. Or his golf game.

Until *The Aviator*, most people, if they knew anything at all about Hughes, thought of him only as a crazy old rich guy with bad hygiene. But I always felt that history had been extremely unkind to—and inaccurate about—Howard Hughes. For whatever faults he may have had, this was a person with an extraordinary sense of life. He lived what amounted to several lifetimes, despite his unnecessarily premature death at age seventy-one.

So, bottom line, Hughes's life instructs me not to be afraid to try, to go after life, to dream, to follow my heart and my vision no matter what. Not to sit around and lick my wounds if my plane (or my idea) crashes, but to get up and keep dreaming, keep working. Keep going. And to always keep my hair, beard, and nails neatly trimmed.

# CORITA KENT AND THE REBELLIOUS NATURE OF INNOCENCE

# 5.0 MIN.

Charles and Ray Eames loved her. Buckminster Fuller shared the podium with her. Marshall McLuhan endorsed her. Ed Ruscha's work was influenced by her. The Catholic church tried to silence her. Born in Iowa and raised in Hollywood, Frances Elizabeth Kent entered the Immaculate Heart of Mary religious community in Los Angeles at the tender age of eighteen and stayed there as a nun, artist, designer, printmaker, educator, and author for the better part of thirty-two years. During that time, Sister Corita led a quiet revolution that reflected and in some ways rivaled the culture of protest and activism of the sixties. Because it was a revolution that marshaled the power of creativity and, well, okay… I'll say it … love.

The sixties saw an explosion of pop art, posters, and graphic materials as tools for inspiring and galvanizing people, and Corita and her students at Immaculate Heart created some of the most powerful and enduring images of that period. Some of her work even anticipated punk graphics a couple of decades before they came about. Her vision was borne of an openness and curiosity (not to mention insomnia) exemplified by her art department "rules," which I will list here:

Rule 1: Find a place you trust and then try trusting it for a while.

Rule 2: General duties of a student: pull everything out of your teacher. Pull everything out of your fellow students.

Rule 3: General duties of a teacher: pull everything out of your students.

Rule 4: Consider everything an experiment.

41

Rule 5: Be self-disciplined. This means finding someone wise or smart and choosing to follow them. To be disciplined is to follow in a good way. To be self-disciplined is to follow in a better way.

Rule 6: Nothing is a mistake. There's no win and no fail. There's only make.

Rule 7: The only rule is work. If you work, it will lead to something. It's the people who do all of the work all the time who eventually catch on to things.

Rule 8: Don't try to create and analyze at the same time. They're different processes.

Rule 9: Be happy whenever you can manage it. Enjoy yourself. It's lighter than you think.

Rule 10: We're breaking all of the rules. Even our own.

It bears repeating here—this was a freaking nun.

I mentioned that Corita's work influenced Ed Ruscha, and it could be debated that Andy Warhol's fascination with advertising was informed by it as well. More recently, Richard Prince and Jenny Holzer owe her at least a nod of gratitude.

Magazine ads, billboards, signage, and packaging all made their way into her printmaking. Rather than viewing the inundation of commercial communication as "low" or intrusive, she embraced these messages as "almost like contemporary translations of the psalms for us to be singing on our way."

Author and civil rights activist James Baldwin said, "The war of an artist with his society is a lover's war. And he does at his best what lovers do, which is to reveal the beloved to himself, and with that revelation, make freedom real." Sister Corita's work is pregnant with sentiments like "The big G (General Mills' logo) is for goodness," "Handle with care," "Born rich," and "Come alive!" (from the ubiquitous Pepsi campaign of the early sixties). Her personal mantras were things like, "Save everything—it might come in handy later," "Look at everything," "Pretend you are a microscope," and "Look hard." To our overly sophisticated, cynical eyes and ears, these sentiments may seem rather naïve and simplistic, but there is something undeniably powerful about Sister Corita's oeuvre—a Google image search for "Sister Corita" will no doubt surprise you if you're not already familiar with her work. You'll likely see what Eames and Fuller and Ruscha saw in her art. And, if you're at all like me, you'll find yourself charmed by it, wanting to return to such a pure expression and interaction with the world around you—all of it. One of her favorite class assignments was to take her students to parts of Los Angeles with little handmade devices she called "finders" and have them spend all day looking at parts of the city that would have previously been thought of as ugly. Or show a film that Charles Eames shared about India and make the students go home and come up with two hundred questions about the film. She admitted that after the first ten or twenty questions, "you get slaphappy, and you start opening up and expanding. Out of the whole batch, you would get some marvelous things."

Interestingly, Corita approached creative assignments in a similar way to Paul Rand, encouraging her students to never start a project with a content-driven idea, but to first focus on shapes, colors, and whatever interested them visually. She believed, rightly, that this process would eventually produce content. This is, of course, the exact opposite of the ham-fisted approach of most advertising people. She may have been a nun. But Sister Corita was definitely a badass. Amen.

# JULIAN SCHNABEL AND THE NEW NON-AESTHETIC

# 6.0 MIN.

I used to suspect that many modern artists were just enfant terribles trying to see how much they could get away with in the name of art. I always had a private suspicion about Andy Warhol and his aptly named "Factory." The YBAs just seemed to confirm my deepest fears, especially when Tracey Emin was short-listed for the Turner Prize for an installation of ... her bed. She called it *My Bed*. A few years ago, Jim Riswold left Wieden+Kennedy to pursue a second career as a fine artist. When I first saw his dollhouse dictators series, I laughed out loud: *Goring's Lunch*, *Hitlermobile*, *Hitler's Sweetheart*. "Dadaism at its most cynical and subversive," I remember thinking. But then I went to see his Mao show at the Augen Gallery and read an introduction to the exhibit that Jim himself had written—about the bullies in his childhood and how he learned to overcome their terror and cut them down to size with humor and outright mockery—and he had me. The story and meaning behind his work suddenly made sense, given that I knew he was also dealing with the terror of a bullying disease (leukemia).

Which brings me to Julian Schnabel, born in Brooklyn, raised in Texas. Painter, sculptor, filmmaker, co-conspirator (with Ian Schrager) of the Gramercy Park Hotel in New York. I thought him to be a competent and adventurous director (*Before Night Falls*, *Basquiat*, *The Diving Bell and the Butterfly*), but I just wasn't sure about his paintings and sculptures. Unquestionably prolific (he once sold sixty canvases in one year), Schnabel produces work that is rough, childlike, rustic (often repurposing existing "art" or materials, and seemingly repetitive.

Then I discovered his crockery portraits. And—like that Jim Riswold moment at the Augen Gallery—it suddenly all made sense. Julian Schnabel is a beast in earnest. He is not just trying to see what he

47

can get away with at our expense. The crockery portraits are (to me) the soul and pinnacle of his beastliness. Schnabel himself has said, "When I'm painting I start off doing one thing … and end up doing something that I never expected to do." He admits that painting and sculpture are still a mystery to him. Which gives me a context for all that other work— it's almost the labor before childbirth, that is to say, the birth of these haunting portraits of family members, friends, lovers, and celebrities. Schnabel starts with huge canvases and then breaks up all manner of crockery—plates, cups, dishes, bowls—and applies the pieces to the canvas. He paints each portrait directly on top of the broken crockery and somehow it just works. What makes it work are the eyes—piercing, penetrating eyes that seem to look right through you. And the broken pottery communicates something on a very visceral level: the brokenness of humanity, and the beauty in the midst of that brokenness. They are reminiscent of Picasso's *Les Demoiselles d'Avignon* and his use of African masks to convey the beauty and brokenness of the lives of French prostitutes.

How does this very personal analysis of one artist's oeuvre relate to a new non-aesthetic? I'm afraid that the answer is just as personal and anecdotal, but it's all I've got (and, of course, I realize that I might be wrong). Several months ago, the *New York Times* magazine referred to Portland's Ace Hotel as "the hippest hotel in the country." Being a devoted "hotelie" (restaurant fanatics are referred to as "foodies"), I had to go check out the Ace. I also wanted to see the new Stumptown café adjacent to the hotel. I introduced myself to one of the hotel's owners, who seemed delighted that I had read the *Times* quote and offered to give me a tour of the property. After seeing the various rooms, library, and lobby, I asked him who the architect was. He said that there was no architect, which made total sense because the hotel is devoid of any of the polish that you would find in a Morgans, Kor, or even an Andre Balazs property. Everything was rough, repurposed, and unrefined. This threw me into a bit of an existential crisis, because I had to admit that I like the polish of a Starck-designed hotel—the Clift in San Francisco, the Delano in Miami. The *Times'* new version of hipness made me feel old, like I had suddenly become the establishment. The same way I felt when Émigré and David Carson came along and declared the end of classic typography/legibility. Then came a sequence of three interlocking events that, together, helped me arrive at a slightly revised worldview:

Event #1: I dove deeper into Julian Schnabel's work and emerged with the above epiphany about his crockery portraits.

Event #2: I saw the film *Helvetica* by Gary Hustwit. I watched slack-jawed as some of my favorite designers inadvertently debated with some of my least favorite designers about the role of typography and form in communications. I say "inadvertently" because they were all interviewed separately, but Hustwit deftly casts, interviews, and edits designers who have clearly opposing viewpoints—some within the same firm.

Event #3: While I was watching *Helvetica* with my daughter (hey, she seemed interested), we heard a crashing of glass coming from the direction of my office. I paused the film and ran upstairs to find my Donny Deutsch plate in a hundred little pieces on the floor. I had received that plate as a gift from my friends at Deutsch LA, with whom I had worked closely over a two-year period of intense growth. Donny had been named Advertising Leader Of the Year by the WSAAA and a big gala was

49

planned in his honor. I was invited to attend and sat with my buds from the L.A. office. To announce the event, a poster was created featuring past winners of the award (which included Lee Clow) on those cheesy Franklin Mint plates, the ones you see in *Parade* every week with Shirley Temple or Elvis. The signed "Forever Donny" plate used for the shoot was put up for auction on eBay by one of the creative directors at Deutsch, who called and asked me to "bid up" on the plate, and that he would pull the auction at the last minute. So I bid up. But when the bidding got up to about $3,500 I began to get nervous. "What if they don't pull it?" The auction was about to end and I was the high bidder at somewhere in the neighborhood of $3,699. I won the auction. But eBay, seeing all the "@deutsch.com" e-mail addresses, busted us, and I was off the hook. My friend was kicked off eBay for six months, and I wasn't allowed to bid on or sell anything for a month. At the Leader of the Year dinner, the Deutsch folks gave me the plate in exchange for my trouble. And now here it laid on my office floor, shattered. Donny Deutsch, the poster child for slick ad men everywhere, was history. So much for "Forever Donny." But that's when it hit me: like Julian Schnabel's broken crockery, the new aesthetic is something of a non-aesthetic. Like it or not, the polish and refinement of corporate America is experiencing considerable backlash—a pendulum swing. Why else would Paula Scher of Pentagram "blame" the Iraq war on *Helvetica* (albeit with her tongue jammed into her cheek) while Gary Hustwit subtly cuts to the work displayed behind her, revealing several pieces set in Helvetica 75 Bold?

51

# ~~THE HANDSOME WRITING OF~~ ~~FYODOR DOSTOEVSKY~~

# 3.0 MIN.

In *Designers Don't Read*, I shared my view that designers tend to make good writers, due to the fact that they are (often intuitively) involved in the editing and organizing of material down to its most potent, digestible form. Maybe that's just the kind of writing I enjoy reading the most: potent and digestible. Direct and immediate. Sans adverbs.

For my money, there is no more sophisticated, economical, or visceral writer than the Russian novelist Fyodor Dostoevsky. The word that always comes to mind when I think about his writing is "handsome." All of his writing is handsome, including *The Brothers Karamazov* and *Notes from the Underground*. But if you want a taste of writing at its most handsome, pick up *Crime and Punishment* and just start reading anywhere. I promise you: guaranteed inspiration.

Some people get Dostoevsky confused with Leo Tolstoy, author of *War and Peace* and *Anna Karenina*. While *Anna Karenina* is a lush and hauntingly beautiful work of fiction—and maybe even the perfect novel— I still see Tolstoy as the Beatles to Dostoevsky's Led Zeppelin. Both tell epic stories: Tolstoy's span years, Dostoevsky's days. His adventures take place mostly within the soul of his characters, and you find yourself simultaneously identifying with and trying to wriggle out of identifying with his flawed, often repugnant characters.

Hemingway cited Dostoevsky as a major influence. James Joyce credited him with inventing modern prose. Nietzsche said that "he belongs to the happiest windfalls of my life." But the reason I include him in this volume is simple: reading him will make you a better writer. It will inspire you. It actually has the power to make you a better communicator.

His biography reads like fiction. Pretend it was you instead of him: you're born in 1821 in Moscow. You grow up in an abusive home, your dad's a retired army surgeon and a raging alcoholic. Your mom dies when you're fifteen, so you and your brother are shipped off to prep school in St. Petersburg. Two years later, your father's such a charming guy that he's murdered by his own employees. At the St. Petersburg Academy of Military Engineers, you suck at math but you start reading Shakespeare, Hugo, et al. You graduate from the Academy as a lieutenant but decide that what you really want to do is write. You publish your first novel at twenty-five, followed by several short stories. You're diagnosed with epilepsy. At twenty-eight, you're arrested for being part of a benign socialist group and sentenced to death. You spend eight months in solitary confinement and then face a firing squad in a mock execution intended to teach you a lesson. This is followed by four years of hard labor in Siberia. Upon release, you get married and launch a literary magazine with your brother; it fails. You start another magazine; it fails. Then your wife dies of tuberculosis, followed by your brother three months later. Already on the brink of financial ruin yourself, you decide to take on your brother's debts, as well. (At least you have integrity.) Unfortunately, you also have a serious gambling addiction. So you have to scramble to write your next few masterpieces at a manic pace just to collect your advance checks from your publisher.

No wonder your words are so explosive, like they're just spilling onto the page. No wonder your writing is so emotive. So efficient.

So handsome.

# LOUIS I. KAHN: WAS IT WORTH IT, LOU?

# 4.0 MIN.

If you haven't seen the 2003 documentary *My Architect*, it's one you might want to own—if only for the rare footage of some of the most amazing structures ever built. But it's especially meaningful if you've ever found yourself stretched between the realities of being an artist in a highly competitive business and the desire to have a family and a life outside of said highly competitive business. The film was written and directed by Nathaniel Kahn, Louis Kahn's illegitimate son. That sounds so bad: illegitimate. How about "his son from a woman other than his wife." That doesn't sound much better. How about just "his son." (Incidentally, Kahn had a daughter from yet another extramarital relationship, in addition to a daughter with his wife, Esther.)

The narrative of the film is the younger Kahn's attempt to get to know his long-deceased father through his buildings and interviews with a handful of the architect's former colleagues. It's poignant and heartrending at times, but what comes through is the obvious reverence that Nathaniel—and pretty much every person who ever knew or hired or sat under Kahn—has for the architect's legacy. Even though that legacy did not necessarily encompass a conventional balance of work and life. In other words, one could easily conclude that Kahn's personal life was a bit of a disaster. Arguably the most important American architect of the past half a century, he died alone and penniless in a bathroom in New York's Penn Station.

As Nathaniel Kahn undertakes his journey to understand his father, we are introduced and reintroduced to his father's oeuvre, which is as remarkable for its limited number of projects as it is for the unbelievable scope and scale and impact of those that were built. A professor of architecture at Yale until 1957, Kahn's career didn't really take off until he was fifty. But when it did, it was nothing short of meteoric. Commissions for art galleries, libraries, churches, residences, and large-scale public buildings followed—all of them iconic and timeless, some of them utterly breathtaking. Recommended: do an image search for the Yale University art building, Exeter Library (especially the interiors), the Salk Institute, the Indian Institute of Management, and the National Assembly Building in Bangladesh.

Kahn combined a deep, philosophical, almost spiritual understanding of architecture with a respect for the classical principles inherent in ancient monumentality—at a time when European modernism, with its rigid, restrictive minimalism, eschewed all references to the past. The result was an entirely new architectural vision. An artistic, poetic vision. One that not only influenced a whole generation of architects (I. M. Pei, Frank Gehry, Norman Foster, and one of my current heroes, Tadao Ando), but, as in the case of his works in Bangladesh and India, inspired and ennobled entire countries. There's a powerful moment near the end of *My Architect* when Nathaniel Kahn interviews a man who worked with Kahn on the construction of the National Assembly Building in Bangladesh. The man is recalling the impact that this building had on the beleaguered people of his country and is so deeply moved that he can barely continue. This serves as a turning point in Nathaniel Kahn's odyssey. He begins to realize the truly lasting impact of his father's work, and it's hard not to conclude that the architect was truly a great man. Not perfect, but great. It seems to even be somewhat healing for Kahn's secret son, providing a context for his father's life beyond his neglect and skewed priorities.

Now, this might all seem rather esoteric if you haven't seen one of Kahn's buildings up close, or watched the movie, or studied his work. But it will all come into focus if you should ever find yourself in Southern California and have an afternoon to spend at the Salk Institute in La Jolla. When you stand in the middle of the center courtyard, between the two symmetric study towers, and gaze out on the narrow channel of water that runs down its central plaza into pools of water below, you feel like you're in a cathedral—with the Pacific Ocean and the sky above it as much a part of the site as the concrete and teak and glass. And it seems impossible that any building could inspire such awe. But it does. And you find yourself forgiving Louis Kahn for being a sucky father and probably an even suckier husband. You find yourself being grateful that one man could somehow realize a vision like this here on earth. You also find yourself wanting to go hug your kid.

# THE BERN PORTER CONTINUUM

# 4.0 MIN.

You know that fine line between genius and insanity? Bern Porter knew it—pretty intimately.

Porter was born in Maine, educated at Colby College and Brown University, contributed to the invention of television, worked on NASA's Saturn V program, published Henry Miller's first (and most controversial) novels, and authored more than eighty books of his own. He was a scientist and a poet, a thinker and an artist, a craftsman and an activist.

His career as a scientist was as tragic as it was illustrious. I alluded to his contribution to the development of TV; Porter worked for a company that was experimenting with the use of colloidal graphite to conduct electrons within the interior walls of cathode ray tubes. He and his colleagues visualized television as a breakthrough for democratizing education not as an advertising platform. Whoops. But the bigger whoops, the experience that impacted his life—and, ultimately, the lives of so many others—was his involvement in the Manhattan Project. During World War II, the government had teams of scientists working independently in different parts of the country, the end of their efforts withheld from each team for secrecy. Porter was recruited to work in the physics department at Princeton and was later sent to a huge industrial plant in Tennessee where they were separating uranium on a massive scale—for bomb production. But Porter and his colleagues speculated about the creative potential of nuclear energy for heat, fuel, and medicine. Until that first week of August in 1945, when Harry Truman gave the order to drop "Little Boy" and "Fat Man" on Hiroshima and Nagasaki, ending the lives of more than two hundred thousand people, most of them civilians. Porter later said that it was writing and publishing that helped him hold onto his sanity in the wake of such a devastating misuse of his talent and intellect.

To give expression to his angst and remorse, he began pursuing new forms of art. "Sciart" was Porter's vision for a fusion of technology and art that predated the Mac by a few decades. He pioneered what we refer to today as "found art," collecting his raw materials each week from the trash bins of the local post office. Porter also became an unheralded leader in the burgeoning concrete or visual poetry movement.

In his biographical manifesto, *I've Left*, Porter outlines his ideas for fusing technology and art, technology and architecture, technology and literature; in his musings about "Scithe" or science and theater, however, his rambling takes on an almost eerie prescience. He predicts the theater of the future as a communal environment where the audience members are also the cast and the producers, or "feeders," as he calls them: "Image after image in epic form is called up, put over and realized in this three dimensional theater of idea, aspect, attitude, suggestion and the concrete wherein the extraordinary, the magic, spontaneous redirects ambitions, wills and urges; this special language which transforms the mind's versions of happenings into events to be perceived, this world of absolute gesture free of written scripts, scored music, dated choreography, theater noises and props which is the idea itself."

Porter conceived of this in the late sixties. But, to me, it sounds like a pretty precise and articulate description of the YouTube phenomenon, where the audience is now the cast and director and producer of these "spontaneous … events to be perceived." He gives the underlying aim of this communal theater experience, "whose first and only objective is to bring people out of themselves and face to face with the reality which is and most certainly out of the stagnation and boredom that engulfs them." He calls this experience "pure theater." I think what he envisioned was

62

content without advertising—basically, his original vision for television. Bern Porter lived a long ninety-three years, and it's probably safe to assume that he was driven for many of those years by a sense of regret and a Jean Valjean–like compulsion to make up for his inadvertent wrongdoing. I actually don't think that's a bad motivation. If marketers and advertising people suddenly realized how much harm they have done to people's intellects and self-respect over the years and decided to devote the rest of their lives and their talents and experience to enhancing the lives of others, maybe we'd be a little closer to Porter's "pure theater." Or maybe they'd just shutter their advertising agencies and go back to school to study design.

# ~~FRANÇOIS ALLAIRE~~ ~~CAN HELP YOU BECOME~~ ~~A BETTER DESIGNER~~

# 4.5 MIN.

I grew up in Canada, which means that I grew up playing ice hockey. It kind of goes with the territory, along with beer and donuts and socialized medicine. But I was one of those odd individuals who actually chose to stand there and let people smack these disks of frozen, vulcanized rubber toward me as hard as they possibly could. And here's the crazy thing: I really wanted them to hit me—I'd actually be sad if they didn't. I was a goalie.

The position has changed significantly since I donned the pads—probably more than the game of hockey itself has. It requires far more athleticism to play goal today, along with a sophisticated set of skills and techniques and body mechanics. The worst goalie in the NHL today is likely to be more skilled than the league's best goalie even twenty years ago. Maybe not as exciting to watch, but definitely more capable of keeping that little black puck out of that big white net (the pipes are red). There's one person who is probably more responsible for this change than any other, and chances are good that you've never heard of him. Even if you're a hockey fan. Or a Canadian.

François Allaire was not a professional hockey player. He actually grew up wanting to be a goalie coach—before there even was such a thing. He got his BA in physical education from the University of Sherbrook, became an avid student of the game and particularly of the position, reading everything he could get his hands on, traveling to Europe to observe goalies there, and challenging every convention of the way the position was played—right down to the design and materials of the equipment that goalkeepers wore. He basically developed an approach that would revolutionize the way the position was played at every level and in every country. And it first began to manifest itself in 1984, when

he began working with someone you probably have heard of, whether you're a fan or a Canadian or neither: Patrick Roy, considered by most hockey aficionados to be the best to ever play the position, was Allaire's first case study, and a brilliant one. I mean "brilliant" in ice hockey terms, not in quantum physics terms. But definitely brilliant—especially when you consider that Roy almost single-handedly won the Stanley Cup (hockey's top prize) for the Montreal Canadiens at the ripe old age of twenty.
He went on to become the most dominant goalie in the game of hockey, shattering record after record and winning every award the sport can bestow on a player. I mean, he really was the Wayne Gretzky, the Michael Jordan, the Tiger Woods of goalies. And, as it turns out, there actually was quite a bit in the way of physics involved in Allaire's approach. Allaire evaluated the way a goalie moved in the net, where he was positioned, what kind of conditioning he would need to optimize his puck-stopping abilities—even if only by the smallest of increments.

Just in case anyone doubted Allaire's impact on Roy's mastery of his position, Allaire repeated his magic in Anaheim with a young goalie named Jean-Sébastien Giguère—who went on to become his team's most valuable player and helped the unlikely Disney-owned franchise become the Stanley Cup champions in 2007.

So, what can François Allaire teach a creative person that could potentially revolutionize the communications world? First of all, he teaches us that it can be done, wherever and whenever it is actually attempted. That by questioning the conventions of how something has been done for years, we can find new ways of approaching it, simply by being aware, observant, ambitious. Allaire has written several books on goaltending, preseason physical preparation, and sports psychology. One of the things he encourages athletes to do is to study their successes. Whenever they have a good game or practice, he asks them to determine what made it successful. He asks them to look for clues: how they mentally prepared, what they ate, when they went to sleep—again, just being aware, observant, and a little ambitious. Caring enough to pay attention to what makes a great project great and a crappy project crappy, and then consciously avoiding those things that resulted in crap. After so many years of success, you'd forgive François Allaire for sitting back and collecting his paycheck and not really continuing to push himself to ask the same questions that he did when he started. But when asked whether he has anything new to learn, the Ducks' goalie coach said, "Always. The game evolves. In the last five years, I've changed my training because of all the changes. Every two years, I will put something new in my system or exercises. New principles develop. It's a great time to be coaching—very interesting things are happening." He'd make a great creative director.

# SIX DEGREES OF ALEXEY BRODOVITCH

# 5.0 MIN.

I'm going to assume that you're already pretty familiar with the Russian-born artist, designer, photographer, and educator Alexey Brodovitch. You probably know him as the long-term art director for *Harper's Bazaar*. And for good reason: he almost single-handedly invented the modern fashion magazine. You've no doubt seen the famous image of Brodovitch surveying the spreads of a particular issue as if they were frames in a giant storyboard. Which makes total sense if you have ever flipped through a vintage *Harper's Bazaar* from the forties or fifties: they have an almost cinematic flow to them, and I swear that many of his spreads would hold up today in terms of pure elegance and visual impact. I started collecting old *Bazaar* back issues a few years ago, and some of them are just stunning—in part because of Brodovitch's taste level and exacting eye, but also because he was able to elevate the magazine to almost the level of a printed gallery, commissioning work from artists like Salvador Dali, A. M. Cassandre, and Man Ray and helping to launch the careers of Irving Penn, Richard Avedon, and so many others—right there on the pages of a women's fashion magazine.

Advertising legend Hal Riney (creator of Bartles & Jaymes as well as an entire genre of wine and beer advertising) once said that "the best insurance against mediocrity is hiring the best possible vendors." In his world, that meant hiring Joe Pytka to shoot his commercials and maybe Elias Arts to score the music. For Brodovitch, it meant being so ambitious about what he wanted *Harper's Bazaar* to become that he refused to settle for anything less than "world class," both in terms of what the publication looked like from cover to cover, as well as the quality of the work from his creative collaborators. While he was adept at nurturing and cultivating creative personalities over the years, he was also fierce

69

in his willingness to edit and crop their work to achieve the impact he was after. "Astonish me" was his constant challenge and mantra to his appreciative and often intimidated students over the years. And he expected no less from himself, his vendors, and his magazine.

In my work with design firms big and small, I have seen sparks of this kind of Brodovitchian thinking. Some of the larger firms have in fact become large by thinking this way—by thinking beyond their market, beyond their category even. And you can see the trajectory of some of the newer firms and almost predict with some certainty those destined for rapid growth. They think big. They don't allow themselves to be defined by perceived limitations. "The client will never buy that" is not a phrase you hear spoken at these places. And if the budget really is an issue in terms of hiring the "best possible vendors," they work even harder and smarter to find "the next Joe Pytka" or "the next Richard Avedon."

I have been working with a small start-up firm based in Portland, Oregon. About eight or nine people, which is tiny in comparison to the Pentagrams and the Landors and the JDKs of the world. But they don't think tiny. They only want to do world-class work for world-class brands. And so they treat every assignment as if it was the most important, most visible project of their careers. And by that, I don't mean that they are temperamental, out-of-touch divas; rather, they try to elevate each project and get their clients to see its potential—both in terms of the project's impact on their business as well as its cultural and aesthetic and even internal (morale-building) possibilities. They make believers out of their clients, and the results are rewarding—on a number of levels. They recently turned a relatively inconsequential PR project for Nike Running into

70

a bit of a movement, winning international awards and sending ripples of inspiration throughout Nike, even as far as Nike's ad agency.

The enemy of this Brodovitchian worldview, in my opinion, is the "argument of presumptive realism." I hope you don't work at a place where you hear it a lot, but it goes like this: "Sure, that may have been fine for (Alexey Brodovitch, Hal Riney, Nike, or insert example of someone doing things correctly here). But let's be realistic. We are not (Alexey Brodovitch, Hal Riney, Nike, or someone doing things correctly)." The argument is intended to appeal to your sense of reality, to reason, but what is so often overlooked by the nervous middle manager or the lazy account person who resorts to the Argument of Presumptive Realism is that *Harper's Bazaar* was a real magazine with real business objectives, Riney was a real advertising man with real clients, Nike is a real company with real investors and very real budgets. What sets famous, successful brands apart from obscure, struggling ones can be reduced to one fundamental value: ambition. Not the Porsche-driving, Rolex-wearing, eighties kind of ambition, but the kind that says, "We are only going to be here for a while, so why don't we invest everything we do with real meaning? Why don't we make every communication we put out there a gift? Why don't we stop waiting for 'the perfect opportunity' and make this one as perfect as it can possibly be? Why don't we stop making excuses for our mediocrity and use our talents and our influence to make this package, this commercial, this poster something special?" I honestly believe that this was the driving force behind the life and work of Alexey Brodovitch. I think if he were alive today he would expect us to respond to this challenge. I think he'd probably just add, "Astonish me."

71

# KEM WEBER, MODERNE-IST

# 4.5 MIN.

Why is it that some of my favorite people have made-up names? Peretz Rosenbaum ("Paul Rand"). Alisa Rosenbaum ("Ayn Rand"—oddly, no relation to "Paul," despite the coincidental before-and-after last names). Paul David Hewson ("Bono"). And here's one that'll surprise you: Allen Stewart Konigsberg (Yup, "Woody Allen"). In all but one of these examples, we can probably chalk it up to some lingering anti-Semitism that existed in the early part of the last century in this country. Sad, but apparently true.

What an odd introduction to a chapter about a German-born designer who traveled to San Francisco in 1914 to work on the German pavilion for the Panama-Pacific Exposition and was stranded there when World War I broke out. Karl Emanuel Martin (Kem Weber, as he became known, his first name cleverly consisting of the initials of his actual name) was refused permission to return to his homeland; instead, he became a U.S. citizen and one of the key figures in American Modernism, particularly on the West Coast. An industrial designer, furniture designer, and architect, Weber came on the scene at what might have been the most interesting and pivotal point in American design history. In the ten or so years following the International Exposition of Modern Industrial and Decorative Arts (whence we eventually derived the term "art deco") in 1925, a bit of an aesthetic showdown was unfolding between the influences of European design, both from the French decorateurs and the Bauhaus "machines for living" functionalists. The battle lines were being drawn between the austerity of the International style and the ornamentation of the French decorative arts of the period. The economy played a key role in this conflict as well, with the luxury and high cost of craftsmanship associated with the excesses of art deco, and the functionality and affordability of mass production reflecting a more democratized and accessible aesthetic. Weber was one of the pioneers of this latter movement.

There seems to be a common thread—besides weird, made-up names—that unites many talented and visionary designers through the ages: the desire to push their work down to the widest possible audience. You can see that in Frank Lloyd Wright's "Usonian" phase and in the apparent eagerness of contemporary design stars like Philippe Starck and Karim Rashid to create everything from timepieces to toilet plungers for mass-market retailers like Target and Fossil. But top designers from the twenties and even up through the sixties had a similar democratic bent. Raymond Loewy, Walter Dorwin Teague, Marcel Breuer, Gilbert Rohde, Eero Saarinen, Charles and Ray Eames—they all designed their share of affordable furnishings, housewares, and knickknacks. I own a bunch of them. And I wouldn't if they hadn't.

Kem Weber, working as he did at the juncture of art deco and the International style, developed a more streamlined approach that combined functionality with just a hint of whimsy and a decidedly Machine Age aesthetic. His furniture designs, like Breuer's and Rohde's and other American modernists (Donald Deskey, Wolfgang Hoffmann, et al.), incorporated a lot of tubular steel and lacquered wood—but there was also an indoor/outdoor functionality to a lot of it as well. Ironically, the one piece of furniture that Weber is best known for, the "Airline" chair introduced in 1934, exploited the lightweight flexibility of molded plywood—more than a decade before Eames would perfect its use in his more famous and ubiquitous plywood lounge chair.

One of Weber's big patrons and clients was Walt Disney, who not only ordered a hundred or so Airline chairs for his offices in Burbank, but also commissioned Weber to design the entire complex, inside and out. If you've ever visited the reproduction of Uncle Walt's formal office at Disneyland's Main Street Opera House, you've seen some of Weber's fun, elegant "moderne" work. A confession: Disney's office is still one of my favorite attractions at the Happiest Place on Earth, a personal idiosyncrasy that my family (thankfully) tolerates every time we visit.

This actually provides some forensic evidence as to what it is that appeals to me about American modernism, specifically the Streamline Moderne expressions of the twenties, thirties, and forties: it was—forgive me—fun. It was playful, hopeful, exuberant. It wasn't all Germanic austerity. Efficient yes, streamlined yes, but with finishes and materials that gave it a sense of mischief. Precisely what I enjoy about—forgive me again—Starck's work. But if you survey other icons of modernism that have stood the test of time, you can see a thread of playfulness and humanity woven into the functionality, whether it's a piece of furniture or a building or an automobile or a logo. Even the most severe. Reminds me of the tension held up by the late great David Ogilvy when he oftentimes quoted an old Scottish proverb: be happy while you live, for you are a long time dead.

# THE BECHERS: ONE MARRIED COUPLE WHO KNEW HOW TO KEEP IT INTERESTING

# 2.0 MIN.

There is really no such thing as a boring project or client—only bored creative people. Case in point: Bernd and Hilla Becher, who met while attending the Dusseldorfer Kunstakademie in 1959, married in 1961, and worked together for the next forty years.

I first became aware of the Bechers work during an exhibit at MoMA, and I have to say that when my partner and I had our postmortem at the end of the day to discuss which pieces stood out to us during the course of the day, their photography was still very fresh in my mind. But here's the thing: we're not talking about nudes or tricks or even techniques really; their body of work over four decades was dramatically singular. Their subjects were industrial buildings and structures, including water towers, blast furnaces, and concrete cooling towers throughout Europe and America.

The Bechers were fascinated by and passionate about "buildings where anonymity is accepted to be the style," and there is something extremely powerful about seeing these somewhat clinical "documentary" images presented the way the shooters intended: organized into grids and literally owning an entire wall of the gallery. At first glance, the exhibit looks like the same image repeated over and over again—shot and framed identically. Except that your eye detects subtle differences from image to image, from structure to structure. That's when you realize what must have captivated them: the subtle diversity and functionality of uniformly designed objects. The similarities and differences fascinate, and you see the inherent beauty of the functional design of each structure— and of the photographs themselves. You and I could have passed by these industrial façades many times and never have seen what the Bechers saw. But you can't help but be drawn into the drama that the

77

Bechers captured with their large format camera. Do an image search and you'll see exactly what I mean. And maybe, just maybe, the next time we are tasked with a seemingly dull or uninteresting assignment, we'll remember Bernd and Hilla Becher, and that even the most mundane subjects and categories have some inherent beauty and story—if we are willing to look for it and put it through a design process that respects functionality and the form that serves it. Moreover, for those of us in long-term relationships, perhaps if we are able to explore and discover some kind of passion—however simple—that we both share, maybe, just maybe, we'll have as enduring and interesting partnership as the Bechers did.

# WALTER PAEPCKE: ~~HURRY,~~ ~~SHARE THIS CHAPTER WITH~~ ~~ALL OF YOUR CLIENTS~~

# 4.0 MIN.

Alternate title: Client as Hero

When you think of the unusual juxtaposition of "client" and "hero," you might be forgiven for automatically conjuring up an image of Steve Jobs in his trademark jeans, running shoes, and black, long-sleeved mock turtleneck. After all, he almost single-handedly pulled his brand baby from the fires of mediocrity and propelled it back into the stratosphere (and beyond), utilizing his secret weapons of product innovation and design— both industrial and graphic. Whenever design critics write or discuss "dream clients," the conversation often seems to gravitate toward Thomas Watson, Jr., who was president of IBM from the early fifties until the early seventies. He was, after all, the captain of industry who famously said, "Good design is good business" and hired Paul Rand to practically baptize the entire IBM culture in his rigorous design process (while simultaneously creating one of the most powerful and enduring corporate identities in the history of business). Even Rand bemoaned the paucity of clients like Watson near the end of his career.

But before Thomas Watson, Jr., and a few years after Lorenzo the Magnificent (the Medici family member who was a patron of many of the artists during the Renaissance), there was Walter Paepcke, a marketing executive at the Container Corporation of America during the 1930s.

In addition to his role at the Container Corporation of America, Paepcke founded the Aspen Institute, hiring Bauhaus designer Herbert Bayer to create the identity and posters for the institute. His affinity for the work of the Bauhaus was evidenced again when he financed László Moholy-Nagy's relaunch of the American New Bauhaus in Chicago. This led to projects and collaborations with other former Bauhaus figures:

81

artists Paul Klee, Wassily Kandinsky, and Josef Albers as well as architects Walter Gropius, Mies van der Rohe, and and Marcel Breuer.

But perhaps his greatest contribution was the one he made at the Container Corporation of America. Paepcke was nothing less than a patron of great design; he believed it was one of the highest values a company could possess. But he didn't just talk the talk. One of my favorite designers gave me a beautiful oversized book a few years ago titled simply *Great Ideas*. The book is a collection of advertisements and promotional materials that the Container Corporation of America commissioned, approved, and produced over a period of twenty-five years. Not only was it one of the longest-running and most popular marketing campaigns in America, it was remarkable for the who's who of design hired to create it. Recognize any of these names? Bayer, Rand, Chermayeff, Glaser, Bill, Munari, Matter, Aicher, Bass, Burtin, Brodovitch, Lustig, Hofman, Federico? Amazing. And so was the work. (The book is appropriately called *Great Ideas*, not *Good Ideas*, although that was also the theme of the campaign.)

Now, how many clients do we know who could fill a book with great ideas that they were involved with—even if they wanted to? Maybe a pamphlet.

I had the rare privilege and pleasure of working with a Paepcke-esque client for close to ten years. Chris Dinsdale was one of the world's foremost authorities on cheese marketing (his dad Owen even consulted the Swiss government on how to sell cheese in the United States). But more importantly (at least to me), he was one of the best and most ambitious clients I have ever met—ambitious not just from a sales perspective, although his contribution to the Tillamook Cheese brand was nothing short of meteoric over those ten years, but in terms of supporting great work and attempting to make every communication with Tillamook's consumer a "gift." He (and his predecessor Gary Sauriol) supported me working with some of the best designers in the country: Steve Sandstrom, Jon Olsen, Bob Dinetz, Fredrik Averin. And he supported our unconventional process, which resulted in some extremely interesting and adventurous communications (see *www.austinhowe.com*). Sadly and suddenly, Chris died a few years ago. And, to put it nicely, the gifts stopped.

At the risk of sounding maudlin (don't worry, I'm not going to tell you to go hug your client), I guess I want to remind us of how rare and precious it is to have a client who respects other humans enough and the creative ethos enough to approve what might be called great advertising. Or, as Walter Paepcke put it, "Great Ideas."

Third possible title for this chapter: Walter Paepcke, Patron of Design or Patron Saint?

# JOHN MELIN AND THE SPIRIT OF WHY NOT

# 7.0 MIN.

If you ask my dear friend and frequent collaborator (and, not coincidentally, the designer of the Designers Don't series), who his biggest influences were and are, Fredrik Averin will name two people. One you know and one you don't. The one you know is Paul Rand. The one you don't (unless you are from a Scandinavian country, or Rick Poynor) is John Melin.

Melin was a largely self-taught graphic designer, who was quietly blurring the lines between advertising, fine art, and industrial design decades before the term "cross-fertilization" even entered the design community's lexicon.

Born in Malmo, Sweden in 1921, Melin attended art school for a couple of years and worked as a decorator for a Swedish fashion retailer before getting hired to work in the art department of an advertising agency in Malmo.

One of his first assignments was to design a newspaper ad for a Swedish vanilla brand. Now, there's something about young creative people when they are just starting out, and this is particularly true of designers who are asked to create advertising early on: they feel as though they need to make an ad that looks like an ad, that sounds like an ad, that feels like an ad. Like other ads they've seen. Many junior designers would phone a project like this in and just throw something together quickly, because, after all, "It's only a boring newspaper ad." Not John Melin. He thought about how to communicate one of the benefits of this product in a memorable way, and then ignored at least one of the traditional boundaries of advertising. He somehow convinced the agency, the client, and the newspaper to mix vanilla with the printing ink, which made the ad actually

85

smell like vanilla. (It also made the printing room smell like vanilla for years afterward.) I think we need to stop for a second and appreciate this feat (we have 5.0 minutes for the entire chapter, after all).

This rookie.

Convinced his elders at the agency.

And the client.

And the newspaper.

To mix vanilla with the ink.

And they did it.

It was a brilliant idea, but you know there had to be just as much brilliance employed in selling it through. As George Lois once said, "95 percent of being a creative person is defending and protecting the work." With all due respect to Mr. Lois, that other 5 percent can be a real bitch. But Melin came up with the idea, and then defended and protected it. Maybe it was just the inspired naïveté of a young designer new to his craft. Maybe it was beginner's luck. But somehow I don't think so, because Melin managed to maintain this approach throughout his entire career. For the sake of justifying the title to this chapter, let's call this approach "the Spirit of Why Not." Why not mix vanilla with the ink?

As it turns out, Melin's willingness to explore new creative vistas wasn't just limited to the content of a piece. Fredrik explains, "For John, it never seemed to be about the medium itself, but more about how an idea could open up the door to another medium." Asking "Why not?" about every dimension and expression of that idea.

Why Not, in this context, is not really a question, although it probably starts out as one. It probably starts out as something akin to "What if?" But, by the time it becomes a fully formed Why Not, it has morphed into more of a commitment. And there is ample evidence that John Melin made that commitment over and over and over again throughout his career, probably long after he had learned that there would always be someone in the room with a litany of reasons why this or that thing could not be done. This spirit comes through loud and clear on nearly every page of his monograph, till Exempel. The book is a revelation, both in terms of the freshness of his work and its consistent quality over a long career.

Just a few examples:

Why not make an out-of-home poster for a museum with the headline printed in wet glue sprinkled with cress seeds, so that the headline will actually sprout, grow, and wilt over time.

Why not package beer glasses in cardboard boxes featuring original artwork (which had never been done before).

Why not make a catalogue cover for a MoMA exhibit called *The Machine* out of sheet metal (decades before Madonna's *Sex* came along).

To beat a horse that was probably dead halfway through *Designers Don't Read*, this is one of the primary reasons I prefer working with graphic designers rather than advertising art directors: they're just more playful, less conventional, and they're generally looking for new forms, new ways of communicating an idea. The best ones are all about the idea. But the "idea" in a designer's mind is vastly different from an "idea" in an art

87

director's mind. It's broader, more encompassing, and less about the gag or a perfectly constructed punch line. Of course, I'm generalizing, but you get my point: the best kind of creative partner is one who might more accurately be called a co-conspirator. Someone who is constantly asking "What if?" about every aspect of the piece, and then, once a beautifully logical and hopefully surprising solution has been arrived at, is answering with "Why not?"

Melin did have a co-conspirator: his long-time creative partner, artist, and illustrator Anders Österlin. They worked as a team for decades. They were known as Anden and Handen, Swedish for "the spirit and the hand." No doubt they provoked and inspired each other, approaching each new assignment with a mischievous Spirit of Why Not.

We could use some of that spirit today. Oh sure, occasionally, it pops through. But it takes a force of will and a modicum of creative ambition that few of us are willing to marshal. It makes me think of something Bob Kuperman, the former president of TBWA\Chiat\Day, once said: "Every great idea began with a meeting where somebody said, 'No fucking way.'" And that makes me think of all the meetings over a sixteen-year period where Frank Lloyd Wright had to repeatedly, doggedly convince Solomon Guggenheim, a battery of New York city officials, and even the exhibiting artists that his bold, cylindrical wonder should be built on Fifth Avenue. And that makes me think of Frank Gehry and his use of crumpled paper and aerospace software, and the fifteen or so years that it took him to finally realize the Disney Concert Hall in Los Angeles. And that makes me think of all the times I have given up on an interesting idea after the first evidence of pushback. And that makes me think that I should redouble my efforts to maintain a Spirit of Why Not. And that makes me think, once again, of John Melin. And how I'd like to change the title of this chapter to John Melin and the Commitment of Why Not. And stop beginning sentences with "And."

# ALMOST EVERYTHING YOU NEED ~~TO KNOW ABOUT AYN RAND~~

# 5.0 MIN.

What do you know about Ayn Rand? What do you need to know?

Let's see: you probably know that she wrote *The Fountainhead*, an iconic novel loosely based on Frank Lloyd Wright's life and career. Maybe you've seen the 1949 King Vidor film version, with Gary Cooper's note-perfect depiction of the irascible Howard Roark. You might know that she wrote the epic *Atlas Shrugged*; you may have even tried to read it once or twice. Perhaps you know her as a devout atheist and philosopher, and you may even know that she had a handle for her particular brand of rational self-interest: "Objectivism." Did you know she was born Alisa Rosenbaum to a Russian Jewish family? If the name change scratches an itch somewhere in your consciousness, it's probably due to the fact that another Rosenbaum—Peretz—also changed his (obviously) Jewish surname to Rand. Yup, Paul Rand was born Peretz Rosenbaum. No relation, except in their souls. Both overcame anti-Semitism and unconventional educational backgrounds to change the world in a significant way. Both were, well, kind of extreme in their views.

What do I want you to know about Ayn Rand? I want you to know that she courageously challenged the intellectual status quo, taking on the decidedly unchallenged sacred cow of altruism with an Emersonian view of man as prime mover and master of his own destiny. She espoused a fierce sense of personal responsibility and a rational approach to life, renouncing magical and religious thinking and man's role as victim or second-hander. I want you to know that she was a human being, and, as such, imperfect and wonderfully inconsistent in her own personal life. I want you to know that despite her own personal foibles she had intellectual integrity for days and a radically high view of man—and woman. I also want you to know that her philosophy, while seeming "evil" and "selfish" to many, makes much more sense than those same critics are willing to acknowledge. She challenges our notions of capitalism and work being inherently evil and bad. She turns them on their head. She makes us, literally forces us, to think. For ourselves.

I remember quite vividly my first brush with an Objectivist—one of my first employers. In the midst of a semi-heated discussion or negotiation about all the extra hours I had been logging during a particular pitch, I made the mistake of saying something to the effect of, "I'm doing all this for the company." He looked me square in the eyes and echoed one of Rand's familiar themes: "Don't do this 'for the company.' Do it for yourself. And if it's good for you and it's good for the company, that's called capitalism." Or, as Rand might put it, laissez-faire capitalism. Basically, rational self-interest.

The underlying principle of Objectivism is that in man's dealings with other men, there should be no such thing as "sacrifice." That doesn't mean that doing the right thing or intervening in someone's life won't be difficult or require courage or even personal pain. This was not a license for narcissism. It was all about values. If I value my kids, it is not a sacrifice to spend time with them. If I value their education, it is not a sacrifice to work harder and spend less on myself to put them through college. It is a value that I hold.

Okay, so this is maybe getting a bit too existential for a book about design and advertising. And you may think at this point that I have completely lost it. I will grant you that this is a rather extreme view, but it does foster a greater sense of personal responsibility, originality, authenticity, and—bottom line—it makes you rethink your premises. Which is what we, as creative people, should always be doing.

Ayn Rand moved the world. Was she an extremist? Hell yes. But sometimes it takes an extremist to move the world a little bit further along. Gandhi was an extremist. Churchill was an extremist. Jobs is an extremist. Adam Morgan, author of my favorite book on marketing (*Eating the Big Fish*) calls this "overcommitment," and lists it as a requisite quality to compete in today's overstimulated, supersaturated media environment.

Remember Alan Greenspan, the former Fed chairman? It was said of him that the expression on his face on any given day could cause the markets to go up or down. There was, for a time, a "Greenspan briefcase cam" that focused on the thickness of his briefcase as he left important meetings: a thicker briefcase signaled trouble and the markets would plunge, while a thinner briefcase inspired confidence and the markets would soar. He was thought to be a more powerful figure than any of the presidents he served under. He was a prime mover. For good or ill, a laissez-faire capitalist. But someone, you will have to admit, who changed or at least influenced the world in a significant way. Well, Rand had a small collective of intellectuals and philosophy buffs who used to meet every week at her apartment on East 34th Street in New York. One of those devotees was a young economist by the name of Alan Greenspan.

You might not agree with her philosophy. You may deplore her politics (she would be a libertarian were she alive in today's political landscape). But you can't argue with her impact. Let's suppose for a second that our own philosophy and political leanings are correct and appropriate. Let's assume some balance and compassion and flexibility in our worldview.

All those ducks in a row, let's now consider how we might champion our own causes with the kind of overcommitment that Ayn Rand demonstrated throughout her lifetime.

As LeBron James has explained, "You can't succeed at all unless you're willing to fail." And, in order to fail, you have to try.

I would love it if you re-read *The Fountainhead*. I'd be even happier if you tackled *Atlas Shrugged*. I think you'd be inspired by both works. But, failing that, the main thing I want you to know about Ayn Rand, the "main takeaway," as our briefs might put it, is that she tried. Harder than most.

95

# WILLIAM WEINTRAUB: THE ANOMALY OF THE FORTIES

# 2.5 MIN.

The one great thing about advertising is that it has provided us with an endless number of quirky, iconoclastic mavericks—both on the agency and on the client side of the shiny conference room table. Stories of the Gallo family and their abuse of their various agencies over the years (which I experienced firsthand)[1]; the notorious bully, George Washington Hill of American Tobacco; Charles Revson of Revlon, who infamously burned through no fewer than nine agencies in the span of thirteen years; this is the stuff of legend. But in 1948, the perfectionist Revson met his match in William Weintraub, founder of William H. Weintraub, Inc., after Revlon's previous agency McCann-Erickson reportedly cycled through eighteen different account executives before finally resigning the business. It was said that "Bill Weintraub knew how to handle Revson; he just out-shouted him, and everything was fine." You know the old saying, "Where there's smoke, there's fire"? Well, it seems that the advertising version of that adage is, "Where there's fire, there's talent." Because wherever you find a "quirky, iconoclastic maverick," you're likely to also to find some gifted individuals rallying around their passion. Such was the case with William Weintraub, who not only attracted great creative clients like Dubonnet and Airwick, but also had a bird-watcher's eye for talent, hiring design great Paul Rand and a writer with no background—or interest—in advertising whatsoever, Bill Bernbach. Bernbach and Rand became fast friends and spent their lunch hours visiting art galleries and discussing how their respective crafts could be integrated to create better communication. I wonder if they realized at the time that these conversations would ultimately send a ripple effect through both the design and the advertising worlds that would change the game forever? What's ironic is that these discussions, if they had been caught on tape, might have sounded an awful lot like the conversations I have had with several talented and visionary designers over the past few years. Some sixty years later.

Bernbach's collaboration with Rand was a watershed moment for the man, and, as it turned out, for the industry. When he joined Grey Advertising in 1945, he rose quickly through the ranks and developed another symbiotic creative partnership with designer Bob Gage, a disciple of Paul Rand. Finding it increasingly difficult to make headway with his then-novel "creative team" approach within the stuffy, bureaucratic, and decidedly client-driven (sans "fire") Grey agency (some things never change), he jumped ship with Ned Doyle and Maxwell Dane to form Doyle Dane Bernbach in 1949.

1. One such story involves the elder Gallo brother actually urinating on the agency's storyboards to express his lack of enthusiasm for a particular concept. The same agency finally resorted to pulling up to the Gallo compound in the agency limo, rolling down the window, and handing storyboards to a Gallo employee, who would then run the ideas up to Ernest and Julio. They would "make corrections" and return them to the waiting creative team to go execute. I guarantee that they were well paid for these indignities.

# BILL BERNBACH AND ADVERTISING'S FIRST CREATIVE REVOLUTION

# 4.5 MIN.

The 1960s saw a seismic shift in advertising from pseudoscientific, research-based, account-driven big agencies to smaller boutiques led by heroic personalities. Gone was *The Man in the Gray Flannel Suit*, replaced by the poet, the storyteller, the social commentator. Metrics and research methodology that bordered on quackery were replaced by instinct and personal expression. Almost overnight, advertising began to attract some of the best and brightest minds, and for a brief, glorious moment in their respective histories, advertising, and design were working hand in hand to create some of the most thoughtful and compelling communication you could find anywhere. And leading this charge was William Bernbach, a Bronx-born graduate of New York University who studied English, music, and philosophy—not advertising.

In 1947, two years before Doyle Dane Bernbach was born, Bernbach was swimming decidedly upstream as a creative director at the aptly named Grey Advertising in New York, when he wrote his now famous memo to upper management, a missive that would still ring true today for that agency and for the vast majority of publicly held agencies as well. It read, in part:

> Our agency is getting big. That's something to be happy about. But it's something to worry about, too, and I don't mind telling you I'm damned worried. I'm worried that we're going to fall into the trap of bigness, that we're going to worship techniques instead of substance, that we're going to follow history instead of making it … If we are to advance, we must emerge as a distinctive personality. We must develop our own philosophy and not have the advertising philosophy of others imposed on us. Let us blaze new trails. Let us prove to the world that good taste, good art, good writing can be good selling.

101

Let history record that Grey did not heed this warning. But Bernbach did, and two years later, on June 1 of 1949, Doyle Dane Bernbach opened its doors with thirteen employees and no clients except for one promising lead: Ohrbach's, a discount department store in New York. With artists and writers now working in teams, DDB created smart, witty, beautiful retail ads that also made Ohrbach's cash register ring. Basically, they were doing Target advertising long before there even was a Target. And it happened because one unconventional ad man (heavily influenced by a visionary graphic designer) saw the possibilities of mixing up design and advertising in a fresh, experimental way. Retail had never been seen as a creative opportunity before, but DDB found a way channel their creative energy into a low-interest category. There's something about being hungry that makes that happen.

DDB spawned some of the greatest creative talent of that or any era, but they had markedly different hiring criteria from other agencies. "We don't care what kinds of accounts you've been working on," a DDB house ad read. "We don't care what size agency you're with now. We don't care about your age, sex, college education, or the other questionnaire trappings." This approach meant that it would often take months for someone to get hired, but there was precious little turnover. No one wanted to leave.

Bernbach's new business strategy was simple: do famous advertising. The Ohrbach's work did, in fact, make the phone ring. And on the other end of the line was Whitey Ruben, from Levy's Bakery. The "You don't have to be Jewish to love Levy's" poster series not only became one of the most beloved and long-running print campaigns of all time, but it rescued Levy's from the brink of bankruptcy.

Of course, the client that would ultimately put DDB on the map—and change advertising history forever—was the strange little car from Germany.

The Volkswagen advertising is the stuff of legend, but there was an interesting aftershock to that famous campaign overlooked by most advertising historians. Namely, Porsche. For years, the prestigious marquee has marked the arrival of every "hot" creative agency in the US: Chiat/Day, Fallon, Goodby, Carmichael Lynch. But, for my money, DDB's first series of Porsche ads, designed by Helmut Krone, have never been bettered. I had them on my wall for a while and people would always ask excitedly, "Is that the new Porsche work?" It holds up, because it came from a place of fusion. And fusion always results in inspiration. And inspiration is timeless.

# JAY CHIAT AND THE AGENCY ~~AS BRAND~~

# 3.0 MIN.

"Your car has a home when you bring it to Cone."

– *Tagline for Cone Chevrolet, written by Jay Chiat, circa 1960*

One of the most famous and influential advertising firms in history had rather inauspicious beginnings. Jay Chiat & Associates and Faust/Day were two small, relatively sleepy advertising agencies in Southern California in the sixties. But then, nearly every advertising agency in Southern California in the sixties was small and sleepy—or a service outpost for a big east coast agency.

When Tom Faust decided he wanted out of the $5-million agency he had founded with Guy Day in 1962, Day placed a call to Chiat, and the two hammered out the details of their merger during a Dodgers game. Maybe it was Jay's vision. Maybe it was his ambition. Maybe it was just the critical mass of doubling the size of his little shop, but Chiat/Day didn't waste any time in becoming the most talked about advertising agency in the country. All from the sunny climes of laid-back Southern California. In 1989, *Advertising Age* named Chiat/Day "Agency of the Decade."

Two books have done an excellent job of covering Chiat/Day's meteoric rise: *Chiat/Day: The First Twenty Years*, written by my old friend and former Chiat/Day copywriter Stephen Kessler, and *Inventing Desire* by Karen Stabiner (who was given unusual access behind the scenes at the agency). So I don't feel the need to cover that ground. What I'm more interested in here is how this upstart agency changed not only the geography of advertising, but how Chiat and Lee Clow and a handful of other like-minded "pirates" managed to build a brand that became almost as famous as the clients they represented. And some of those

105

clients—Apple, Nike, Porsche, and Energizer among them—were pretty damned famous, in large part because of the advertising created by the maverick agency.

In many ways, Chiat/Day was a product of the eighties—more specifically, a product of California in the eighties. Chiat's management style, which today would be considered obsessive-compulsive, was rule by fear. Whenever any of the offices heard rumblings of the possibility of one of Jay's infamous visits, everyone would scurry about, cleaning up their offices, sharpening pencils in the conference room, and steeling their self-esteem against a potential Jay attack—which might only take the form of him forgetting your name. But underneath this paternal intimidation was a much deeper, more powerful influence. A feeling of destiny, of pride—the pride of working at the best advertising agency in the world. There was very little turnover at Chiat/Day and it was well known that one would be required to take a pay cut to work there. All manner of self-promotional pieces and stunts were attempted (my favorites: Lee Clow's original "Hire the Hairy" campaign and Dick Sittig's "Dick for Brains" piece), and there were files full of résumés with notes attached that read simply, "Will work for free." Halcyon days, those. In their pre-Gehry days, whirring about on the second floor of the Biltmore Hotel in downtown Los Angeles, people worked all night and all weekend—happily. After all, they weren't making ads; they were changing the world.

# SPEAKING OF CALIFORNIA RIFFRAFF: WILLIAM KESLING

# 4.5 MIN.

There is an old Yiddish saying that can be loosely translated, "God loves riffraff." And I admit that I kind of do, too. I guess what I love and respect is scrappiness, courage, determination, balls. And one person who embodied those qualities was the architect William Kesling, who built "thousands" of homes, stores, and apartments around Southern California in the thirties and forties. I put the quantity of his completed projects in quotations due to the controversial and highly questionable accuracy of his math. However, what he lacked in veracity he more than made up for in chutzpah. And natural talent.

Kesling moved to Los Angles in 1920 and worked his way up from carpenter's helper to superintendent in a few short years. By 1923, he had become a general contractor, and five years later, he opened up his own practice, Kesling Modern Structures. Far from feeling inadequate for his lack of a proper architecture education, Kesling took great pains to know more about designing and building, to be more up on the latest materials and methods, than many of his college-trained peers. The architecture establishment, however, did not take him seriously because of his unconventional career arc and lack of pedigree.

Kesling's first residential project was a spec house. Scraping together his meager savings (and with a little help from his mother-in-law), he purchased a steep hillside lot in the quaint Silver Lake section of Los Angeles. The Streamline Moderne gem cost far less to build than the modern residences being constructed by Richard Neutra and Rudolph Schindler, Kesling's better-known competitors at that time.

When the project was completed in 1934, it attracted so much attention that Kesling became hot. Hotter, in fact, than Neutra and Schindler.

Commissions came pouring in, and soon Kesling's "scintillating modern structures" were sprouting up all over West Hollywood, Sunset Plaza, Pasadena, Westwood, and the San Fernando Valley. He also designed and built the sleek modernist Desert Club in Borrego Springs. By 1936, William Kesling was prospering, due in large part to the fact that he had actually delivered a modern home for people of modest means. He did have several Hollywood luminaries as clients, but his claim to fame was that he was able to deliver a truly modern home for under $3 per square foot while Neutra was building structures at an astronomical $10 per square foot.

With the sheer volume of work he was attempting to do and oversee, Kesling had leveraged himself to the hilt, leaving his business exposed—one setback and the whole thing threatened to come crashing down. The setback came in the form of rising costs, dwindling profits, and an obnoxious client by the name of William Greene who doggedly pursued the architect's untimely demise.

Granted, William Kesling was a far better designer than he was a businessperson. Admittedly, he took on way more than he could handle. And there was enough of the huckster in him to qualify him for "riffraff" status. Very much like Preston Tucker, his automotive equivalent: brilliant and flawed.

What is the lesson of William Kesling and Kesling Modern Structures? There are probably several. But perhaps the most poignant one is about the importance of brilliant creative visionaries being grounded by brilliant business people. Like Michael Jager and David Kemp at JDK. Like Steve Sandstrom and Jack Peterson at Sandstrom Partners.

An even more powerful and eloquent lesson lies in the "scintillating structures" themselves. A few years ago, some friends of mine in Los Angeles took me on a tour of important modernist buildings in the area. I had seen many of the Wrights and Lautners before, but they showed me several of Kesling's residential projects—including two that they happened to own. The one in the Hollywood Hills was originally called the Rivero House, and they told me how they stumbled onto it without realizing at first that it was a Kesling. Apparently, it had been reskinned at some point with an Asian façade. When they investigated a little bit further, it turned out to be this gorgeous moderne cottage with dramatic views of Hollywood and Los Angeles below. They lovingly restored it to pristine original condition.

Now, some of my more hardcore modernist designer friends out there are probably rolling their eyes at my penchant for the art deco and moderne aesthetic and getting ready to remind me that "form follows function" and "all ornament is crime." And they're probably right, except for one sliver of logic that I refuse to let go of: what if part of the function of a particular building is to express optimism, joy, romance, or playfulness? Do my austere modernist friends view Frank Gehry's work as decorative or unnecessarily ornamental? I don't think they know quite what to do with it. Or Philippe Starck's work. Or Karim Rashid's. Or even Rem Koolhaas's. There is humanity expressed there. There is a sense of time and materiality that I love. You couldn't and wouldn't build a Kesling structure today, unless you were building an exhibit for Disneyworld. But the indomitable spirit of William Kesling lives on. Long live the talented riffraff.

# BILL CAHAN IS STILL HUNGRY

# 4.0 MIN.

A number of years ago, I was working as a creative director at an advertising agency and we decided that it was high time we revisited how we packaged and presented our work. I launched an initiative to see how some of the best design firms in the world packaged and presented theirs, reasoning that design firms (more so than advertising agencies) would probably have a sophisticated approach to self-promotion. I made a list of my favorite twenty or so design firms, went through annuals and identified a few more worth contacting, and asked some colleagues if there were any others to whom I should reach out. Then I had them all send their materials.

The notion was to see who did the best job of presenting themselves—and then have that firm help us with our own self-promotion. After all the metal boxes and faux leather books with screws had been rifled through, there was one package that stood out from the rest. It was a stack of annual reports, posters, brochures, ads, and booklets, all wrapped rather roughly in makeready sheets that read, "Maybe great products aren't about beautiful design." It certainly helped that the work inside was some of the freshest, smartest, and most sophisticated communication I had ever seen assembled in one place. The package had come from Cahan & Associates in San Francisco.

Like most iconic leaders, Bill Cahan is complicated. Opinionated. Fearless. Driven. But, above all, he is restless and easily bored. Maybe that explains why, after only five years at Anshen & Allen, he left a promising career as an architect to launch a graphic design and branding firm in San Francisco. That was in 1984, and over the next twenty-five years, the man and his firm literally transformed at least one dimension of design and business communications. While the

113

firm became famous for its annual reports (Cahan was the first design firm principal to be invited on CNBC and CNN to talk specifically about "ARs"), it was the firm's unique and somewhat obsessive process that elevated some of their work to the level of fine art. Cahan's work can be found in the permanent collections of the Chicago Athenaeum Museum of Architecture and Design, the Cooper Hewitt National Design Museum, the Library of Congress, and the San Francisco Museum of Art.

My first collaboration with Cahan was an eye-opening experience—first when I saw how expensive they were, and then when I observed their creative development process firsthand. I have to tell you that I've had the good fortune to work with some of the most creative, sophisticated advertising agencies in the country: Wieden, Chiat, Crispin, BBDO, Saatchis, Deutsch. But none of them came even close to the thoroughness and exhaustiveness of Cahan's process. Seriously, I had never seen any company delve so deeply or hungrily into the client's culture and every existing document or datum about that company and its category. It was crazy. Hours, days, even weeks of collecting, note taking, thinking, and analyzing—before a single design was even remotely considered. And there, lurking about, was Bill Cahan—ever the catalyst—questioning them, poking them, provoking them to go deeper and to think harder about what this client was all about and how they could communicate that in the most memorable way possible.

The firm was launched in 1984 as a "strategic design agency that would be different from others in two main ways: 1) We would work harder to educate ourselves about our clients' businesses, and 2) We would look for fresh, intelligent approaches to implementing strategic solutions." They followed that original charter with remarkable success.

In many ways, the lesson of Bill Cahan's life and career to this point parallels that of Ian Schrager's. Schrager famously superimposed what he learned from his wildly successful and notorious Studio 54 onto the hospitality industry, creating the first chain of well-designed boutique hotels, where the lobby essentially became the new "club." Interestingly, once he had perfected the concept and others had copied and drafted off it, he jettisoned the Morgans Hotel Group to pursue a new vision: hotel as gallery with artist Julian Schnabel. Both Cahan and Schrager created successful hybrids by changing the model of the category they were entering. Both seem to want to break that model and move onto something new. Both men seem to almost always be hungry to change things up and set new standards.

In 2009, Cahan surprisingly handed over his entire book of business, his contacts, and his database to his partner and another staff member to pursue yet another venture. When he is ready to unveil his new vision, I suspect that it will be yet another interesting hybrid of some sort. I, for one, am anxious to see what he's going to do for an encore.

# JOSEF MÜLLER-BROCKMANN AND WHY A WRITER GIVES A CRAP ABOUT THE GRID

# 4.5 MIN.

Confession: I freaking love Josef Müller-Brockmann. I love just about every piece he ever created—at least the ones we know about. And I love his whole grid system dogma. I love his use of Akzidenz-Grotesk. And I love his seemingly repetitive poster designs for Musica Viva and Zurich Tonhalle. I love his patchwork education and that he jumped around from illustration to graphic design to exhibition design to advertising and back to graphic design again. And I could not in good conscience have compiled a list of individuals who have inspired me without including Herr Müller-Brockmann.

That said, I will leave the heavy lifting of the designer's life and work to the excellent biographies written by Kerry William Purcell and Lars Müller. Chances are good that you've read at least one of them, and I hope you've treated yourself to Müller-Brockmann's own *History of the Poster*. If you really want a full immersion, I also highly recommend *Grid Systems in Graphic Design*.

Suffice it to say that the Swiss designer thrived on constraints. He even provided his own constraints, as if his clients didn't provide him with enough of them. Ah. Perhaps therein lies a key to his rampant con-straintism: until the late sixties, when Müller-Brockmann began landing larger accounts like IBM and later Olivetti and Swiss Railways, many of his clients were smaller and less likely to interfere with his creative process. Theaters and other entertainment venues are not known for creative meddling or being too demanding—except when it comes to budgets and timelines. They are more apt to deal in the currency of creative freedom. Which may explain in part why Müller-Brockmann's process evolved into such a strict, almost formulaic approach. But here's the cool thing about his work—even or especially some of his more

117

"repetitive" work: there is always such power and visual tension in those posters, even if the various components are relatively similar. The whole of his creative energy and imagination is being condensed and pushed down into those few elements, and it creates an undeniable impact. Think nuclear energy. Compressed energy.

One of my favorite advertising agencies ever to hang out a shingle was OMON in Sydney, Australia. OMON stood for "Only Meaningful Only New." And while the agency only had a short reign, it dominated awards competitions and its principals were all eventually lured away by bigger concerns. One of OMON's brightest stars was David Droga, who eventually became the celebrated creative director of Saatchi & Saatchi in London and now has his own hybrid firm, Droga5. I judged the Clios a few years ago with David and told him how much I admired OMON's work. He shared some of the behind-the-scenes oddities of the place (some of the staffers legally changed their names to tilt the numerology in their favor), and one thing about their process struck me: apparently, the writers and art directors were separated. This was in almost direct opposition to the way agencies have operated since Bill Bernbach first teamed them up in the sixties, during what was widely considered the "creative revolution" in advertising. OMON had the writers generate a specific number of ideas against a creative brief and then turn those ideas over to the art directors. In turn, the art directors were expected to hone and plus those ideas and develop them further. No back-and-forth. No mutual epiphanies. It is said that the art directors were so angst-ridden because of the slight represented by these apparent constraints that they worked even harder to make those ideas stronger and push them even farther. The result was the creation of some of the most interesting—and most beautiful—ads I have ever seen. Very powerful stuff indeed. And, not unlike Müller-Brockmann and his grid, the agency's self-imposed constraints freed them to infuse those strictures with as much imagination and creativity as they could muster within themselves.

Danny van den Dungen of Experimental Jetset in Amsterdam defends the firm's frequent use of Helvetica by explaining that being creative and imaginative is not about finding cool new experimental typefaces, but rather about the idea and how the type is used to communicate that idea. If the font is in some ways a given, the freshness and originality of the idea becomes more important.

Which leads me to what may appear to be an obvious point: we, as creative people, do not really have any excuses for producing uninspired, unimaginative work. We can never "blame it on the client." We can't show our work and say things like, "This would have been super cool except the client made us do this and so …" Because, in the final analysis, the very constraints that send many of us running to the obvious solutions can instead inspire us to push the work even farther. If the client kills one strong idea, come back with a stronger one. Or, better yet, three or four stronger ones. Embrace the limitations of a small budget. Embrace the client's wife who has definite opinions about the use of teal (but try not to embrace her with the client in the room). Embrace Helvetica, or at least a short list of clean, legible, simple typefaces. And blow the idea out like a mother …

Josef would have wanted it that way.

# ~~MITCH HEDBERG: THE MAN WHO WOULD HAVE BEEN KING OF COMEDY~~

# 4.0 MIN.

A story is told about Will Ferrell's reaction to Sacha Baron Cohen's *Borat* when the movie first came out. Apparently, after seeing it at the theater, Ferrell went home and wept. When his wife Viveca asked him what was wrong, he said between sobs, "I'll never be that funny."

Now, the star of *Anchorman*, *Elf*, and *Talladega Nights* is arguably the funniest man alive. So that was high praise indeed for the star of *Da Ali G Show*, *Borat*, and *Brüno*. But, for my money, the funniest comedian to ever grab a microphone was a painfully shy, often high, and highly unlikely stand-up by the name of Mitch Hedberg, originally from Minnesota. Many of you will know him, but I am always surprised by the number of people who don't. Sadly, the reason for Hedberg's relative obscurity is his tragic death at age thirty-seven of an overdose—just as his career was beginning to take off and some were calling him the heir apparent to Jerry Seinfeld. He appeared on *The Late Show with David Letterman* no fewer than ten times. He was in the movie *Lords of Dogtown*, did an episode of *That '70s Show*, and released three CDs of his caustic and sometimes painfully absurd brand of comedy. Hedberg rarely looked at his audience, often wearing sunglasses on stage and letting his long hair fall down in front of his face. He always seemed nervous and self-conscious, but was able to turn that awkwardness into part of his act, often screwing up punch lines, deciding to tell a joke backwards, or commenting on his own delivery ("That joke was retarded" or "I don't know what I was trying to pull off there").

So, half of Mitch Hedberg's act was about his unconventional delivery (sometimes accompanied by a double bass), but the other half was his writing: brilliant and blatantly obvious observations and inspired non-sequiturs. I'll share a few of my favorites:

121

I wish I could play Little League now. I'd kick some fucking ass. I'd be way better than before.

An escalator can never break. It can only become stairs. You would never see an "Escalator out of order" sign, just "Escalator temporarily stairs. Sorry for the convenience."

My apartment is infested with koala bears. It's the cutest infestation ever. Way better than cockroaches. When I turn on the light, a bunch of koala bears scatter. And I'm like, "Hey, hold on fellas. Let me hold one of you … and feed you a leaf."

I want to be a racecar … *passenger*. Just the guy who bugs the driver. "Say man, can I turn on the radio? You should slow down. Why do we have to keep going in circles? Can I put my feet out the window? Man, you really like Tide."

My lucky number is four billion. That doesn't come in real handy when you're gambling. I'm not addicted to gambling, I'm addicted to sitting in a semicircle.

I haven't slept for ten days, because that would be way too long.

I bought myself a parrot. The parrot talked, but it did not say it was hungry, so it died.

If I had a dollar for every time I said that … I'd be making money in a very weird way.

And so on. It would have been very interesting to see where Mitch Hedberg could have gone had he not had that self-destructive bent that seems to drive and ultimately destroy so many comedians.

**122**

He was one of those performers who could be called an "artist" because his talent just cut through the fog of alcohol and drugs and insecurities. He was just flat-out talented. Period. And he changed the Seinfeld model of well-spoken, highly polished, likeable boy next door. Hedberg was more of the Lenny Bruce school. With a pinch of Steven Wright and Sam Kinison (minus the screaming) for flavor. The irony of his death was punctuated by two of his more telling insights:

> Alcoholism is a disease, but it's the only one you can get yelled at for having. "Damn it, Otto, you're an alcoholic! Damn it, Otto, you have lupus!" One of those just doesn't sound right.

> I used to do drugs. I still do drugs, but I used to do them, too.

# ~~DON'T HATE ME BECAUSE~~
# ~~I LOVE PHILIPPE STARCK~~

# 5.0 MIN.

Please don't roll your eyes. I know that Philippe Starck is the epitome of the "pop" designer. I know that he is overexposed. I know that many of you don't take him seriously as an industrial designer, or as an interior designer, and definitely not as a graphic designer. But hear me out, because I think there is one thing that we can agree on about Monsieur Starck's oeuvre. First, let me get the basics out of the way—Starck 101, if you will.

Born in Paris, in 1949. Spent a couple of years at the École Nissim de Camondo. At twenty, he went to work as an art director at Pierre Cardin. In the seventies, he focused on interiors and designed a few sweet bars, before being commissioned to design François Mitterand's private apartment at the Élysée Palace in Paris. But his real breakout project was his interior for Café Costes in 1984. That kind of put him on the map. A few years later, he designed the interiors for Ian Schrager's Royalton and Paramount hotels in New York, which launched a long and successful creative partnership between the two iconoclasts. His partnership with the design-centric Italian company Alessi yielded many successful products, but none more famous than his *Juicy Salif*, the futuristic lemon squeezer for which he is probably best known.

Through partnerships with luxury brands like Alessi, Vitra, Kartell, Duravit, Axor, Flos, and Baccarat, Starck has designed everything from teapots to teddy bears, lamps made out of guns to clear acrylic chairs. For more mass-market retailers like Target and Fossil, Starck has done what nearly every great industrial designer since the time of the Bauhaus has attempted to do at some point in their career: push down his work to those of more modest means. Basically, make great design accessible to just about anyone. As much as I would like to have one of his "Haaa!!!"

125

Baccarat crystal floor lamps, I'm not really prepared to dish out the requisite $119,250 to light my office. That said, I fully appreciate my sweetly designed "O-Ring" watch designed by Starck for Fossil (retail price $99). And my $20 Starck toothbrush. And, despite the fact that Schrager jettisoned his original collection of Starck-designed boutique hotels years ago, I still love walking into the Paramount lobby, past the marble wall covered from floor to ceiling with chrome vases for individual roses. I still love seeing Starck's signature underlit bar and eclectic collection of furniture at the Mondrian and the Hudson. I appreciate the fact that Philippe Starck attempts to inject thoughtfulness, playfulness, and mischief into the most mundane, everyday items and experiences. Juicers, toothbrushes, watches, toilet brushes, bathroom scales, cheese graters, and yes, $120,000 floor lamps.

I mentioned that many product designers have historically gravitated to pushing their work down into a more affordable realm. Frank Lloyd Wright with his Usonian houses. Michael Graves's collection at Target. Going further back, Walter Dorwin Teague and the Eames and Marcel Breuer and Raymond Loewy (who designed everything from locomotives to cigarette packaging). In 2004, the Raymond Loewy Foundation honored Starck with the Lucky Strike Designer Award for his life's work. This was the jury's rationale (not mine): "Philippe Starck is probably the most unusual, quirkiest, and most exciting designer of the past twenty years and is likely to be for decades to come."

My personal mission statement for my career (which I blatantly co-opted from Vincent Van Gogh) is simply this: "Consolation for humanity through advertising and design." In other words, my overarching ambition in everything I do is to create "gifts" for the intended receiver. Something

**126**

they appreciate, enjoy, value. Not just an intrusion or another unwanted product. A gift.

Love him or hate him, it's hard to deny that Starck has made an earnest effort to elevate our experience here on this planet. To make our everyday experience a little bit more special. And, while he has garnered a small fortune doing so, at least he is laughing all the way to the bank. And at least a few of us are laughing with him.

If you have indulged me this far, and you don't mind spending another minute or two on the subject, here is a nonexhaustive list of some of my favorite Starck designs. You can easily find images of them online.

Starck's Greatest Hits*:

Juicy Salif lemon squeezer for Alessi

Louis Ghost chair for Kartell

Delano Hotel for Ian Schrager

Mondrian Hotel for Ian Schrager

Paramount Hotel For Ian Schrager

St. Martin's Lane Hotel for Ian Schrager

Royalton Hotel for Ian Schrager

Clift Hotel for Ian Schrager

SLS Hotel for Sam Nazarian

Starck House for 3 Suisses

*Don't Hate Me Because I Love Philippe Starck*

Asahi Beer Hall for Asahi Breweries

Hudson Rocker for Emeco

Collection Guns lamps for Flos

Zenith Black chandelier for Baccarat

Hugo Boss Boutique

Maison Baccarat, Moscow

Prince Aha Stool for Kartell

Gnomi seats for Kartell

Ceci N'est Pas Une Brouette chair for XO

Monsiegneur seating collection for Driade

The Tooth Stool for XO

Out-In Sofa for Driade

Almost all of his Fossil watches

Almost all of his Axor faucets

Almost all of his Duravit bathroom fixtures

Almost all of his Puma shoes

*In no particular order, and this is only my opinion.

# ~~IN MY HEART, I AM TYLER BRÛLÉ~~

# 1.5 MIN.

I definitely have a few things in common with Tyler Brûlé, the founder of both *Wallpaper*\* magazine back in the early nineties, and, his most recent effort, *Monocle*, a "global briefing" of international business, culture, and design.

Both of us were born in Canada. Both of our families came from Winnipeg, Manitoba. Both of our fathers were professional athletes—his father, Paul Brûlé, played football in the CFL, and my father, Alfred Howe, was a prize fighter. Both of us no doubt caused our dads considerable head-scratching and consternation over our penchant for art and design over footballs and boxing gloves. Tyler became a writer at a young age. I became a writer at a young age. He also launched a branding firm at a relatively young age—as did I. Tyler is obviously passionate about design. I am passionate about design. But, unfortunately, that may be where the similarities end.

Brûlé is an international bon vivant and culture shaper. In 2005, the U.K.'s *Independent on Sunday* ranked him forty-third on its list of most influential gays and lesbians in the U.K. I am—at best—a "gay heterosexual," meaning that I love everything about the gay lifestyle except the sex. Brûlé travels all around the world and publishes an annual list of the world's most livable cities. I live in one of those livable cities (Portland, Oregon) and occasionally sojourn to places like New York, Los Angeles, and once in a great while, London.

Tyler Brûlé launched an amazing, bar-raising, niche-creating magazine that was purchased by Time Warner in 1997. Which means that he probably made a little more money than I did when my partner and I sold our advertising firm in 1996.

But still. We're brothers under one flag. Okay, maybe two flags: the Canadian flag. And the flag that says, "I (heart) design." Except Tyler Brûlé would never have an "I (heart) design" flag.

133

# ADAM MORGAN COULD BE YOUR BEST FRIEND OR YOUR WORST ENEMY

# 5.0 MIN.

Adam Morgan is smart. Scary smart. Not only was he the strategic majordomo for TBWA\Chiat\Day and responsible for brands like Virgin and Apple, but his book, *Eating the Big Fish*, a survey of what he refers to as "challenger brands" (second-rank brands whose ambitions are greater than their resources and are willing to accept the implications of that gap), is easily the best book on marketing and branding I've ever read. Four times. His follow-up book, *The Pirate Inside*, takes the challenger mind-set inside bigger, more complex organizations and shows how even establishment brands can act like challengers. Great stuff. Must-reads.

Adam is one of those odd birds that advertising people call "account planners," a term that Morgan's former employer, Jay Chiat, popularized here in America back in the eighties. Account planning actually had its genesis in London, where a few advertising agencies felt that the role of research within the creative department had become almost completely irrelevant to the entire creative process. As David Ogilvy (a Brit himself) once said, "Like a man uses a lamppost, for support instead of illumination." So, a handful of smart, ambitious creative firms started recruiting psychology and sociology majors from Oxford and Cambridge to come and study their clients' customers—their habits, their feelings about the category and the brand, and so on—and to help uncover insights that could inform and inspire the creative work. The term "account planning" derived from the notion of getting ahead of the consumer, of seeking illumination instead of always putting the consumer in the position of advertising critic after the fact. Not only did account planning result in startlingly fresh and relevant creative work, it also proved to be a powerful secret weapon for winning new business. In addition to an agency's quantitative research capabilities, they were now able to go into a pitch with a new prospective client often knowing more about their customers than the clients did themselves. That's when Chiat decided to import the discipline, and before long, all of the major creative agencies in the United States were employing the practice, often repurposing account people or traditional researchers.

Now, I have to admit, I am a bit of a slave to account planning—especially if the people doing the consumer work are smart. And I have been fortunate to work with some extremely smart planners over the years: Chris Riley, formerly with Wieden+Kennedy and then Apple; Emily Reed, formerly with Goodby Silverstein & Partners; Lisa Grey from QRC (her husband Arnie was one of those early planning pioneers in the U.K.); Jen Urich from Crispin and La Communidad; Daniel Baxter from Sandstrom Partners and formerly with Goodby and Chiat. There have been others, but these planners are all in the "brand neighborhood" of Adam Morgan. And they are all capable of mining the target audience and/or the client culture for insights, a strategy that could totally light your way as you navigate through an assignment where there may be deeply entrenched rules of engagement or indifference or crazy levels of complexity. They also have a slightly more subversive role, which can endear them to you for life: part of their charge is to find ways to help the client trust a piece of challenging creative (assuming that there is strong conviction within the agency that the direction is right for the client). I remember Chris Riley explaining his approach at a place like Wieden: "We do our best to provide the best context and logical platform for the creatives to step off from, but if inspiration strikes,

I'm completely prepared to reverse engineer the brief to support a brilliant idea." I remember thinking, "I love these guys. These planners."

However, as with all good things, there is a danger in leaning too heavily on the strategic underpinnings of even the smartest, most inspiring account planner. Not so much within advertising agencies (frankly, they need all the help they can get), but within design firms. I have seen otherwise brilliant and completely earnest account planners and strategists threaten to rob great designers of the very thing that makes them great: their process. Much of the work of an account planner actually parallels the design process: digging, talking to people, poring over company data, looking at precedents, analyzing, studying interrelationships, exploring possibilities. Great designers do all these things. So do great planners. When the planner unwittingly does the designer's work for him, the designer is relegated to the role of decorator to some degree. It's a tempting business model, for a number of reasons. One, as Chiat proved, it's a tried and true way to get new clients. Two, it seems more efficient: let the strategist wrestle with the strategy and then let the designer make it pretty. But, in that one seemingly small step, an otherwise forward-thinking design firm takes a giant leap back in time and even across the divide into the advertising world—to the days before Bill Bernbach, when writers were the strategists who handed off their ideas to the designers to make them pretty.

Design is a system. A logical system. It is also a process. And I'm not saying there isn't room for huge contributions from smart people within that process, but I do think roles have to be clearly defined. Or the designer will gradually become more and more of a wrist instead of a mind. And the best designers I know are all about the mind. I like to think of design as "beautiful logic." But, to paraphrase something my dad used to say, beauty without logic is like a pig with lipstick.

I still don't really know what that means. Maybe Adam Morgan would.

# HENRY HOHAUSER ALWAYS MAKES ME HAPPY

# 3.0 MIN.

My first trip to Miami was both exhilarating and exhausting. Exhilarating because I had never seen so many structures built in the Streamline Moderne or Nautical Moderne style in one place at one time. Oh, I had the coffee-table books and had seen pictures of all the famous deco landmarks, but I was the biggest geek in South Beach when I arrived to speak to the advertising club there. They were kind enough to ask me which hotel I wanted to stay at, and I was seriously torn: the Delano? The National? The Shelborne? The Carlyle? The Breakwater? The Cardoza? The Dorchester? The Essex House? The Colony? The Delano, recently remodeled by Ian Schrager and Philippe Starck, was booked full, so I made my decision based on one interior detail I had seen (in several books) of the green Vitrolite and chrome fireplace with a Diego Rivera-like mural in the lobby of the Colony on Ocean Drive, reasoning that if this detail was so impressive, the whole property must be remarkable. It wasn't. I checked out as quickly as I checked in when I realized that the fireplace and façade were the only remnants of the hotel's original charm—there was even a TV set in the fireplace. From there, I checked into the National, which was in much better condition. The next night I stayed at the Shelborne. But I didn't actually sleep during the three short days I was in Miami; instead, I stayed up all night, photographing every club, apartment, library, and hotel from every possible angle. I was in deco heaven. And it was then that I learned that the one man responsible for 90 percent of these beautiful, exuberant structures was a graduate of the Pratt Institute in Brooklyn by the name of Henry Hohauser. He moved to Miami in 1932 at the age of thirty-seven and designed more than three hundred buildings in Miami and the surrounding area. I think I saw them all—all the ones still standing, at least. Hohauser's influences were obviously the World's Fairs, the Chrysler Building in New York, and

141

the climate and vibe of South Beach itself. And that is where I have some ground to stand on in terms of my love for this period of architecture. While the International style seemed to fit the gloom and austerity of 1930s Depression-era America, Hohauser's little gems burst with optimism and the hope for a better future. He integrated the materials, colors, nautical themes, and whimsical flora and fauna of the seaside resort to create a singular vision, a style now known as Tropical Deco. He built as if to say, "Come on, people! Look at where you live—it's amazing!" And that sentiment still holds up today, long after *Miami Vice* went off the air and South Beach underwent a massive transformation from drug haven to hot spot. Hohauser and his contemporaries, designers like L. Murray Dixon and Albert Anis, not only created the buildings but gave attention to the aforementioned details—carpeting, terrazzo patterns, lighting, and built-in custom cabinets and furniture. The result is a sense of exuberance, a kind of sense of life, as Ayn Rand might put it. I know that some of my more austere modernist and postmodernist designer friends are not as sympathetic to the Streamline Moderne aesthetic as I am, but that's okay. When I study some of my favorite contemporary architects' work, I see a similar embracing of the materiality, environment, vibe, and time in which we live. A little playfulness, a little optimism, a little whimsy is not a bad requirement for any brief. Otherwise, I fear that we end up with big concrete boxes and a utilitarian strip mall mind-set. So, the next time you're in South Beach, check out some of Hohauser's work, and I dare you not to crack at least a small, knowing smile. Because everything is going to be okay.

142

# ~~SUSAN HOFFMAN IS THE ONLY ADVERTISING ART DIRECTOR IN AMERICA~~

# 5.0 MIN.

Officially, Susan Hoffman is the co-executive creative director of Wieden+Kennedy's Portland office. She is also officially a partner in the agency. Unofficially, I believe, she is much, much more than that. In my estimation (and in the estimation of many of her colleagues over the years), she is the first person to bring Art into Wieden+Kennedy. Certainly, cofounder David Kennedy, the ultimate Zen master, set the stage for her and others to do so. There was an artist lurking inside of him (he retired to pursue sculpting), but Kennedy—for all of his contributions to his agency and the ad world in general—was pretty much just a talented art director and creative director of the Chicago school. There was a crazy degree of magic when he eventually teamed up with copy-writer Dan Wieden and they started working on this little athletic shoe company in Beaverton, Oregon. They did solid, smart, cheeky work for Nike. But I think they discovered what their real gifts were after they launched their agency on April Fool's Day of 1982. Turns out they would excel at identifying, inspiring, and guiding a whole new generation of creative types—more Kerouac and Pollack than Ogilvy and Hopkins. One of their first hires was a feisty young art director who was toiling away at one of Portland's lesser-known agencies. Susan Hoffman was born into the Hoffman Construction family, a dominant Northwest firm. Nothing about her career to this point suggested the creative star she would eventually become, but both Wieden and Kennedy prided themselves on finding uniquely talented individuals and creating an environment in which these individuals could do the best work of their careers. And they had staggering success when it came to this mission: many of their first hires, including artist Jim Riswold and CEO Dave Luhr, stayed with the firm for the rest of their careers. Luhr is still there. So is Hoffman.

145

I remember going to Rich's Cigar Store (the periodical equivalent of Powell's Bookstore, one of the largest in the world) and seeing Susan poring over European fashion magazines. Other advertising didn't seem to inspire her at all. Her work seemed to be more influenced by the worlds of fashion and fine art and foreign films. And to that end, she began to nurture and develop other talent at the agency who thought the same way. Michael Prieve was one such individual, who could be said to have been an actual "art director"—that is, a director of art. His work for Nike and Calvin Klein and Ian Schrager's Paramount Hotel did not look or feel like advertising at all. This was a time when Nike was all about experimentation, and it created an opportunity for several Wieden+Kennedy creatives to become stars in their own right. Even art directors who were cut in the traditional advertising mold began to find a new voice; those who remained traditional found that they did not have as much of a role at Wieden, except perhaps on a few of the agency's more conservative accounts. But, behind it all, pushing and prodding and swearing like a longshoreman, was Susan Hoffman. She literally made a career out of being an art patron. The role of art buyer (there are several at Wieden) became one of the most important functions within the agency, and Hoffman encouraged creative teams to explore the larger creative world for ideas and executions. This non-insular approach is what propelled the Portland agency's exponential success over the next decade. It helped that their clients' budgets allowed them to hire world-class directors, animators, photographers, and artists, but they earned those budgets by pushing the envelope harder than most of the so-called creative advertising agencies in the country.

By the time Wieden brought in Todd Waterbury, a designer from Duffy Partners, and John Jay, creative director at Bloomingdale's, the bar had already been set. Hoffman had already championed collaborations with Tibor Kalman (on Subaru), Steve Sandstrom (on Black Star Beer and Nike), and several other notable designers.

In *Designers Don't Read*, I posited that advertising art directors don't anymore; that is, they don't direct *art*. For the most part, they direct other advertising that they've seen, quite often from abroad. The biggest reason for that is the pragmatic approach of so many American advertising agencies, who are more interested in hiring young creatives (out of schools like "Portfolio Center," where the emphasis is clearly on having a book of finished-looking ads as opposed to finding your unique voice) who can create things that look like other things that are successful at that point in time.

Susan Hoffman is an anomaly in the advertising world. As is John Jay and Todd Waterbury. I repeat, they are not normal. They, and their partners, are more apt to encourage young creatives to "fail harder." They're not as interested in "cool viral ideas" as they are odd, interesting, unique voices and visions. If more advertising agencies took this approach, and, in fact, if Wieden keeps growing in this direction, I might have hope for the agency world. But I worry. I worry that pragmatism and profitability and growth and "keeping good people employed" will deter even "art-full" agencies from the Van Gogh-esque mission of consolation for humanity through art. I worry that the pantheon of traditional advertising gods will win the day, and design will be seen as decoration, an add-on instead of a thorough process and system that needs to permeate the entire agency culture. I'm not even sure that Wieden+Kennedy *knows* that they have more of a design culture than an advertising culture. But somehow, as long as Susan Hoffman is manically flitting about and dropping f-bombs on NW 13th and Everett, I think everything will be just fine.

149

# THERE ARE THINGS YOU DON'T KNOW ABOUT FERDINAND PORSCHE

# 3.5 MIN.

The difference between Porsches and porcupines? Porcupines have pricks on the outside. Yeah, I've heard them all. Even when I point out how timeless and spartan and functional Porsche's designs actually are, I still get grief from most of my designer friends for my affection for the car (particularly the 911, now in its forty-fifth year). "A relic of eighties extravagance," I'm told. But did you know that Porsche designed the original Volkswagen Beetle? You probably did. But I'll bet you didn't know that Professor Porsche was mostly self-taught (with honorary degrees from Austrian and German universities and technical institutions) and that he really learned his trade at the Vienna-based Jakob Lohner & Co., where he designed and built the world's first electric car in 1898. That was followed by the first four-wheel drive electric car, which he debuted at the 1900 Paris World Exhibition as the "Toujours-Contente." Like today, the issues of power and range were somewhat limiting for the electric car, and so—remarkably—Ferdinand Porsche designed the world's very first gas/electric hybrid vehicle, the "Mixte" vehicle/transmission concept in 1901. This is not a typo; we're talking about a true hybrid vehicle—actually produced—more than a hundred years ago. And, not as surprisingly, this particular vehicle was fast, and Porsche himself broke several Austrian speed records driving a front-wheel drive hybrid in 1901. By 1905, Porsche was being honored as Austria's most outstanding automotive engineer, and was recruited to become Austro-Daimler's chief engineer the following year. Porsche received an honorary doctorate from the Vienna University of Technology in 1917 and another from Stuttgart Technical University for his work at Daimler, which was soon to market their vehicles under the marquee of Mercedes-Benz.

Ironically (and you can begin to see an obvious pattern here), in the late 1920s, Porsche had a vision for a small, lightweight Mercedes-Benz vehicle. The concept was not a popular one with the Daimler-Benz board, and not long afterward, they parted company and Dr. Ing. h.c. F. Porsche GmbH was born.

In addition to developing designs for other automakers, Porsche continued to develop his own designs, including his original idea for a lightweight, highly efficient car that was also capable of high speeds.

At the 1933 Berlin Motor Show, German Chancellor Adolf Hitler announced two new programs: "the people's car" (a democratically priced vehicle also known as *Volkswagen*) and a state-sponsored racing program. Sadly, Porsche profited greatly from these and other Nazi-related initiatives, and in December of 1945, he was arrested as a war criminal. He spent twenty months in prison before his son, Ferry, raised enough money from the family business to have him released.

It was at this time that father and son developed the 356. Unable to get financing from banks because they were still under the American embargo, Ferdinand Porsche was undeterred: he took his little rear-engine sports car around to Volkswagen dealers and took orders, asking for payment in advance. More than seventy-five thousand cars were sold before the 911 made its debut in 1963.

One of the most compelling aspects of the Porsche 911 is how relatively few changes have been made to its basic design over nearly half a century. Like a great typeface, the original inspiration holds up generation after generation, with just minor tweaking here and there (think Helvetica Neue). And this is where we actually learn something about design from

Professor Porsche and his legatees. It was said of their controversial design for the first front-engine Porsche, the 928, that it was not designed to be immediately embraced, but that the design would eventually be appreciated even more than an instant hit might be. Other than some interior refinements and the addition of (functional) spoilers, the design did not change significantly from its introduction in 1977 until 1995. Many of the styling cues from the 928 have reemerged in more recent Porsche models, with much of the engineering being repurposed in the franchise-resuscitating Porsche Cayenne, also a front-engine departure for the marque.

Now, as Porsche AG continues to reinvent itself by producing more fuel-efficient and innovative designs, it is one of the healthiest automotive brands in the world. There is something about visionary, timeless, confident, and functional design—even if part of that function is unnecessary performance—that stands the test of time. As well as the test of political turmoil, despotism, imprisonment, financial woes, and massive cultural shifts.

After fifteen years of driving Porsche cars, I am finally surrendering to my conscience and the realities of the economy and getting rid of my little Porsche roadster. Somehow I think that the German car company will do just fine without my brand loyalty. Especially since I'm replacing it with Dr. Porsche's other brainchild: a Volkswagen.

It has less in common with a porcupine.

# MY LIFE IN DESIGN, PART ONE

# 4.5 MIN.

In *Designers Don't Read*, I described how I narrowly escaped becoming the Canadian sausage king by pursuing a career in advertising. At Ad Center, I focused on writing; my day job allowed me to put what I learned into practice as the in-house creative department for Howard Meister, a former racecar driver and owner of a few Porsche dealerships in southern California. I got to know the folks at Chiat/Day, who were handling the Porsche account at the time, and I was able to bring in freelance designers and art directors to help me create the communications for Meister's various companies (he also owned a telecommunications business and a high-end construction company). I had other brushes with designers, and while I was intrigued by their apparent knowledge of typography and art movements and stuff like that, I didn't fully appreciate their process or their role—at least in relation to what I was doing. It wasn't until I was a creative director at an advertising agency in Portland that I had my first taste of bringing a designer into the creative process—early in the process.

Aaron Smith was educated as a graphic designer and a fine artist and had done an internship at an advertising agency, but he didn't even have a portfolio of ads to show me. But he was my first hire, and we not only created some insanely interesting ads and identities and branded materials; we more or less reinvented our whole creative process. Aaron's adventurous spirit (there are many Aaron stories) and inspired naïveté provided a refreshing change from my previous job, where I partnered with award-winning and now famous art directors who limited their creative solutions to those found in annuals—or at least to those that the current year's jury might appreciate. My next hire was also a designer, and more interesting work followed. I kept one foot in the advertising camp,

155

but continued to work with (at least) rebellious or uncharacteristically imaginative art directors as well.

During this time, a new design firm had launched in Portland, called Sandstrom Design. Steve Sandstrom had been a star designer at Nike and more recently had been working as an in-house designer for an advertising agency (ironically, the same agency at which Aaron Smith interned), until he and business partner Rick Braithwaite decided to buy themselves out of that situation and launch their own proper firm. They were an immediate success, and fortunately for me, I got to ride some of it. Our first collaboration (for their identity) won a gold pencil at the *One Show*, and they went on to become a force in the industry, best known for their branding and packaging of Tazo Tea. Over the years, Steve and I collaborated on various projects, usually for my company and sometimes for his. I also collaborated with Sara Rogers, a former Duffy designer and principal of Design Metro, also in Portland. She had never worked on a television campaign before and I thought that was the perfect prerequisite for creating some interesting work for Honda. The TV and print we did for that effort was truly strange and almost cost me the account—except that the dealers saw an increase in floor traffic and concluded that unusual advertising might be a bit of a secret weapon for them. Phew.

It wasn't until I was back at my old alma mater (Cole & Weber, now Cole & Weber United) as executive creative director that the design fire began to burn more brightly in me. For one, I inherited an already kick-ass digital department, and I was also tasked with growing our in-house design component. Studying our parent company at the time, Ogilvy & Mather's BIG (Brand Integration Group), was part of that task;

it left a lasting impression on me. A year later, I was the executive creative director at a firm called Nerve, where I collaborated again with Sandstrom Design on various projects and first came into contact with Cahan & Associates (see "Bill Cahan Is Still Hungry"). I ultimately decided to hang out my own shingle and work exclusively with my favorite graphic designers; I've been doing that ever since.

Despite the fact that I am able to work alongside some of the most talented designers in the country, as a freelance writer and creative director, I sometimes miss the "cause" of working on one brand 24/7. I've learned that I prefer to be "brand monogamous," but I also love being exposed to new firms and new processes. I enjoy helping design firms bridge the gap between their process and advertising. I work with a few small hybrid firms that share my interdisciplinary vision, and that's where I feel like I have the most impact. However, it is my talented designer friends and colleagues who most inspire me, who help me fulfill my personal mission: *consolation for humanity through advertising and design*. And it is for them that I have written this modest volume. My hope is that the little sparks of inspiration that these individual stories provided me with will help them to do even better work. That is, if they actually spend the 154 minutes it will take to read this book.

# THE END

# 0.5 MIN.

# INDEX

# 6.0 MIN.

## Index

163

# Index

# *Index*

167

# APPENDIX

# 9.0 MIN.

"I am still passionate about continuing to rethink
things and going off into uncharted territory."

– *Ian Schrager*

"Fuck."
– *Susan Hoffman*

"When you want to give something presence,
you have to consult nature.
And there is where design comes in."
*— Louis I. Kahn*

"A building is like a man; it has integrity and just as seldom."
— *Ayn Rand*

"Flowers grow out of dark moments."
— *Sister Corita Kent*

"An ashtray is perfect. An ashtray has got life and death."
— *Damien Hirst*

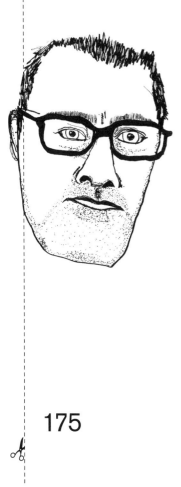

"80% of what everyone's talking about never happens."

*— Jay Chiat*

"Realists do not fear the results of their study."
— *Fyodor Dostoevsky*

"We have to replace beauty,
which is a cultural concept, with goodness,
which is a humanist concept."
– *Philippe Starck*

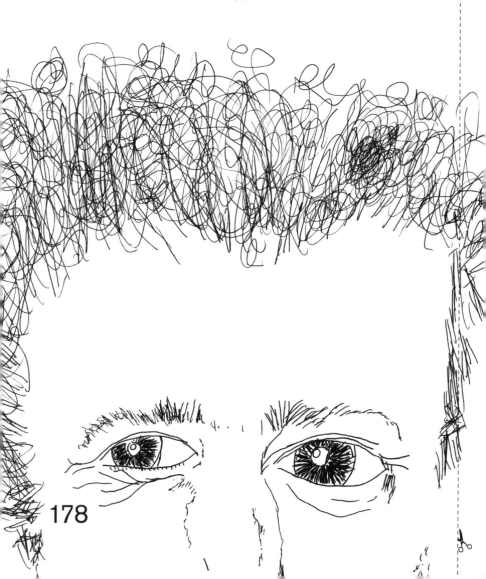

178

"If one does not fail at times, then one has not challenged himself."
– *Ferdinand Porsche*

179

"I was ambitious for the work, and not ambitious for myself."
— *Rachel Whiteread*

"Art has been neglected. Nothing has happened in the field for centuries. Get the subject off the canvas and out into the air. Reverse perspective. Kick in the wall and let the stuff stand alone."

– *Bern Porter*

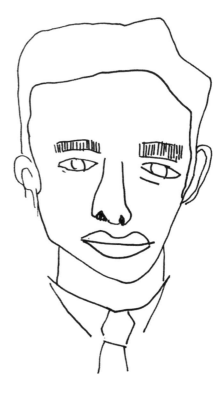

181

"The photographer, if he is to maintain his integrity,
must be responsible to himself. He must
seek a public which will accept his vision,
rather than pervert his vision to fit that public."

*– Alexey Brodovitch*

"A principle isn't a principle until it costs you something."
– *Bill Bernbach*

"Art schools used to put the fear of God into their students
by asking them *"Can you make a living out of that?"*
We wanted just the opposite and simply told
them to make stuff first and then we'd go on from there."

*– Bernd Becher*

"No, of course I'm not in it for the money."
– *Charles Saatchi*

185

"My paintings take up room, they make a stand.
People will always react to that. Some people get inspired,
others get offended. But, that's good. I like that."

*– Julian Schnabel*

"My approach to design is to make the practical
more beautiful and the beautiful more practical."

–*Kem Weber*

187

*Appendix*

"People do not know what they want until a brilliant person shows them."
– *Maurice Saatchi*

188

"I'm not a paranoid deranged millionaire. Goddamit, I'm a billionaire."
— *Howard Hughes*

189

"Only in such a fusion of talents, abilities, and philosophies can there be even a modest hope for the future, a partial alleviation of the chaos and misunderstandings of today."

*– Walter Paepcke*

"I'm sick of following my dreams, man.
I'm just going to ask where
they're going and hook up with 'em later."

— *Mitch Hedberg*

"It's a fact of life, but it's a good fact of life. It's not good
for music if you play the same things over and over."

– *Matt Haimovitz*

"The grid system is an aid, not a guarantee."
– *Josef Müller-Brockmann*

193

*Appendix*

"_____."

*– You*

195

# COMPLIMENTARY
## NOTE AND SKETCHBOOK

# 9.0 MIN.

*Complimentary Note and Sketchbook*

*Complimentary Note and Sketchbook*

*Complimentary Note and Sketchbook*

*Complimentary Note and Sketchbook*

*Complimentary Note and Sketchbook*

*Complimentary Note and Sketchbook*

209

*Complimentary Note and Sketchbook*

213

*Complimentary Note and Sketchbook*

*Complimentary Note and Sketchbook*

*Complimentary Note and Sketchbook*

*Complimentary Note and Sketchbook*

**Books from Allworth Press**